Oven
Only
meals

Quick References

Be sure meat is cooked thoroughly. To test the doneness of oven-baked dishes, use a meat thermometer inserted in the thickest part of the meat with these updated USDA guidelines for minimum cooking temperatures:

145° <u>Whole meats</u> *(including pork)*
Allow meat to rest for 3 minutes before slicing or serving.

160° <u>Ground meats & egg dishes</u>

165° <u>All poultry</u>

Rice For best results in these recipes, use regular long grain white rice unless recipes specify instant or brown rice.

Ground beef For less fat in finished dishes, use lean ground beef.

Printed in the United States of America
by G&R Publishing Co.

Distributed By:

507 Industrial Street
Waverly, IA 50677

ISBN-13: 978-1-56383-412-7
ISBN-10: 1-56383-412-X
Item #7069

Contents

Toss it Together, Pop it in the Oven

These delicious recipes can be thrown together quickly and tucked into the oven for a no-fuss, no-muss home-cooked meal sure to delight your family. There's no need to boil noodles, brown meat or sauté vegetables ahead of time, so you'll have more time for the things you really want to do. When the timer goes off, just pull your food out of the oven and add fruit, salad or bread to complete your meal. With a busy life, what could be simpler?

Make meal prep even easier...

...when you use these convenience items:

- Ready-to-use sauces
- Canned soups
- Pre-shredded cheeses
- Diced ham
- Frozen, ready-to-bake meatballs

- Frozen, fully cooked chicken breast strips
- Canned chicken and seafood
- Instant or frozen mashed potatoes
- Frozen hash brown potatoes
- Frozen or canned vegetables

...when you use leftovers & planned overs:

- Buy a rotisserie chicken for one meal, then shred or chop the extra meat for casseroles.
- Cube or shred leftover Thanksgiving turkey and freeze in small portions.
- When making mashed potatoes for one meal, prepare extra to freeze for later use in casseroles.

Skip the browning — but add color with ingredients like dry soup mixes, paprika, sauces, cheese and colorful vegetables.

Skip the pre boiling — rice and dry pasta will cook just fine in the oven without it. Provide adequate time and added liquid for tenderness.

Skip the sautéing — just add chopped or sliced vegetables to your other ingredients for baked-in flavor.

4

Beef

Beef

Grandma's Pot Roast

serves 6

Ingredients

1 (2 lb.) boneless beef roast (such as sirloin tip or bottom round)

2 medium potatoes, peeled

2 medium carrots, peeled

2 parsnips, peeled, optional

1 onion

¼ tsp. pepper

1 (14.5 oz.) can Italian stewed tomatoes with juice

1 (10.75 oz.) can cream of mushroom soup

1 tsp. minced garlic, optional

Preparation

Preheat oven to 325°. Place beef in a large oven-safe skillet, Dutch oven or roasting pan. Cut potatoes, carrots and parsnips into even chunks. Slice onion into wedges. Arrange vegetables around meat in pan; sprinkle with pepper and top with tomatoes. Spread soup over meat. Stir garlic into ½ cup water and pour around vegetables. Cover and bake for 1½ hours or until meat and vegetables are tender. Before serving, remove meat and vegetables from pan and thicken cooking liquid as desired. Slice beef and arrange on platter with vegetables.

When recipes call for canned soups, bouillon or other salty ingredients, go easy on the added salt.

Vegetable Beef Stew Bake

serves 8

Ingredients

1 (2 lb.) boneless beef
  chuck roast
4 medium potatoes, peeled
3 medium carrots, peeled
8 fresh mushrooms
3 roma tomatoes, peeled
1 C. chopped onion
1 C. sliced green bell pepper

1 bay leaf
1 C. frozen corn, optional
1 (10.75 oz.) can tomato soup
¼ C. flour
2 tsp. instant beef
  bouillon granules
2 tsp. dried Italian seasoning
1 tsp. pepper

Preparation

Preheat oven to 300°. Trim any fat from beef. Cut meat into
1" cubes and place in a 6-quart oven-safe Dutch oven or roasting
pan. Cut potatoes and carrots into 1" pieces. Slice mushrooms in
half. Chop tomatoes. Place potatoes, carrots, mushrooms, tomatoes,
onion, bell pepper and bay leaf into pan with meat. Stir in corn,
if desired.

In a medium bowl, whisk together soup, 1 cup water,* flour, dry
bouillon, Italian seasoning and pepper until blended. Pour soup
mixture over meat and vegetables; stir gently. Cover and bake for
3 hours or until meat and vegetables are tender. Discard bay leaf
before serving.

Dry red wine may be used in place of water.

Beef

Stuffed Bell Peppers

serves 4

Ingredients

4 medium green, red
   or yellow bell peppers
1 lb. lean ground beef
¾ C. chopped onion
¼ C. uncooked white rice
4 T. ketchup, divided

½ tsp. salt
1 tsp. dried oregano, divided
¼ tsp. pepper
1 (14.5 oz.) can Italian stewed
   tomatoes with juice

Preparation

Preheat oven to 350°. Slice the top off each bell pepper. Remove membranes and seeds; set bell pepper shells aside.

In a large bowl, combine uncooked ground beef, onion, uncooked rice, 3 tablespoons ketchup, salt, ½ teaspoon oregano and pepper; mix thoroughly but lightly. Spoon mixture into pepper shells and stand filled peppers upright in an 8" square baking dish.

In a small bowl, mix tomatoes, remaining 1 tablespoon ketchup and remaining ½ teaspoon oregano. Pour over filled peppers. Cover dish tightly with aluminum foil and bake for 1½ hours or until the internal temperature reaches 160°.

Easy Hamburger Oven Meal

serves 6

Ingredients

2 C. diced potatoes
  or green cabbage
2 C. chopped celery
1 lb. lean ground beef
1 C. diced green bell pepper
1 C. chopped carrots

1 (14.5 oz.) can diced
  tomatoes with juice
1 C. sliced onion
Salt and pepper to taste
1 T. Worcestershire sauce

Preparation

Preheat oven to 375°. Lightly grease a 2½-quart baking dish with nonstick cooking spray. In prepared dish, layer potatoes, celery, uncooked ground beef, bell pepper and carrots. Add tomatoes and onion; sprinkle with salt and pepper. Drizzle Worcestershire sauce over the top. Bake for 1½ hours or until vegetables are tender and ground beef is cooked through. Cover with aluminum foil for the last ½ hour of cooking time, if desired.

Variation *Omit bell pepper and carrots; add one 15.5-ounce can dark red kidney beans with liquid and substitute one 10.75-ounce can tomato soup for diced tomatoes.*

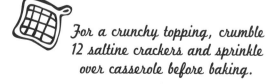

For a crunchy topping, crumble 12 saltine crackers and sprinkle over casserole before baking.

Beef

Meatball Medley

serves 6

Ingredients

1 (6 oz.) pkg. lower-sodium stuffing mix for chicken

Water and butter as listed on stuffing package

1 (10.75 oz.) can cream of mushroom or cream of celery soup

¼ C. milk

12 oz. frozen, fully cooked mini meatballs (about 24)

2 C. frozen mixed vegetables

1 C. shredded Cheddar cheese

Preparation

Preheat oven to 400°. Combine stuffing mix with hot water and butter as listed on package. In a 9 x 13" baking dish, stir together soup and milk. Add meatballs and vegetables, stirring to combine. Top with cheese and prepared stuffing. Bake for 20 to 25 minutes or until heated through.

Variation *For Italian medley, substitute one 14.5-ounce can Italian herb diced tomatoes (with juice) for the soup and omit milk. Use Italian-flavored meatballs and shredded 4-cheese blend in place of Cheddar cheese. Bake as directed.*

Classic Corned Beef Dinner

serves 8

Ingredients

1 T. flour

1 large oven cooking bag (16x17½")

1 (2 to 2½ lb.) corned beef brisket

½ tsp. ground allspice

½ tsp. salt

½ tsp. pepper

1 head green cabbage

1 onion

3 large carrots, peeled

Preparation

Preheat oven to 350°. Pour flour into oven bag and shake well. Place bag in a 9 x 13" baking pan (2" deep). Roll down top of bag and add ½ cup water; squeeze bag gently to mix. Add beef to bag, fat side up. Sprinkle allspice, salt and pepper over meat. Cut cabbage and onion into six wedges each. Slice carrots into sticks. Arrange vegetables around beef in oven bag. Close bag with nylon tie. With a sharp knife or scissors, cut six ½" slits in top of bag to let steam escape. Tuck ends of bag into pan. Place pan in oven and bake for 2 to 2½ hours or until meat is fork-tender. Let stand 10 minutes.

With scissors, cut open the top of bag and carefully remove food; stir remaining juices in bag to blend. Discard top leaf from cabbage wedges. Slice beef and serve with vegetables and juices.

Beef

Savory Meatloaf with Roasted Veggies

serves 6

Ingredients

1½ lbs. lean ground beef
¾ C. quick-cooking rolled oats
¾ C. finely chopped onion
½ C. chili sauce
1 egg
1 T. Worcestershire sauce
2 tsp. minced garlic, divided
1¾ tsp. dried thyme, divided
½ tsp. salt

¾ tsp. pepper
6 medium potatoes
6 medium carrots, peeled
1 onion
2 T. olive oil
Additional salt and pepper, optional
Additional chili sauce, optional

Preparation

Preheat oven to 350°. In a large bowl, combine uncooked ground beef, oats, chopped onion, chili sauce, egg, Worcestershire sauce, 1 teaspoon minced garlic, 1 teaspoon thyme, salt and pepper; mix thoroughly but lightly. Shape mixture into a 4 x 8" loaf on the rack of a broiler pan; set aside.

Quarter the potatoes. Cut carrots into ¾" pieces. Cut onion into thin wedges. In a large bowl, combine vegetables with olive oil, remaining 1 teaspoon garlic and remaining ¾ teaspoon thyme; toss to coat well. Line a jelly roll pan with aluminum foil and spread vegetables over foil; sprinkle with additional salt and pepper, if desired.

Place meatloaf pan on upper oven rack; place vegetable pan on lower rack. Bake meatloaf and vegetables for 50 to 55 minutes or until meat is fully cooked and vegetables are fork tender. Brush meatloaf with additional chili sauce during last 10 minutes of baking, if desired. Let meatloaf stand 10 minutes before slicing.

Beef

Cheesy Tater Tot Casserole

serves 6

Ingredients

1 lb. lean ground beef
2 T. dry onion soup mix, or to taste
2 C. frozen mixed vegetables
Pepper to taste

Onion salt, optional
1 (10.75 oz.) can Cheddar cheese soup
1 (5 oz.) can evaporated milk
16 oz. frozen tater tots

Preparation

Preheat oven to 350°. Crumble uncooked ground beef evenly over bottom of an ungreased 7 x 11" baking dish. Sprinkle soup mix over meat. Top with vegetables and season with pepper and onion salt, if desired. Set aside.

In a medium bowl, stir together cheese soup and evaporated milk until well blended. Spread soup mixture evenly over vegetable layer in baking dish. Arrange tater tots in a single layer on top until covered. Bake for 1 hour or until mixture is bubbly and meat is cooked through.

Variation
Substitute ½ pound ground sausage for half the ground beef. For extra vegetables, use one full 12-ounce package frozen vegetables (about 3 cups).

Beef

Scrumptious
Short Ribs

serves 4

Ingredients

1 onion
2 green onions
1 medium carrot, peeled
2 celery stalks
2 to 3 tsp. minced garlic
1 tsp. dried thyme

1 C. red wine or beef broth
½ C. soy sauce
1 T. sugar
Pepper to taste
3½ lbs. beef short ribs
3 medium potatoes

Preparation

Thinly slice onion and green onions. Chop carrot and celery. In a large roasting pan, combine all onions, carrot, celery, garlic, thyme, wine, soy sauce and sugar; stir until well blended. Season with pepper. Add ribs and toss to coat well in marinade. Arrange meat in a single layer in marinade, cover tightly and refrigerate for 6 hours or overnight. Turn meat several times during marinating. Remove pan from refrigerator 30 minutes before baking.

When ready to bake, preheat oven to 400°. Bake ribs and vegetables in covered pan for 1 hour. Reduce oven temperature to 350°. Remove pan from oven and turn ribs; add water to pan as needed to maintain cooking liquid. Cover and return to oven to bake 1½ to 2 hours longer. Meanwhile, peel and quarter potatoes. Add potatoes to pan for the last 40 minutes of baking time, cooking until tender.

Super Simple Baked Ziti

serves 8

Ingredients

24 to 26 oz. spaghetti sauce
1 (15 oz.) container
   ricotta cheese
1½ C. beef broth or stock
2 C. shredded mozzarella
   cheese, divided

¾ C. grated Parmesan
   cheese, divided
12 oz. uncooked ziti pasta
24 frozen, fully cooked
   meatballs, slightly thawed

Preparation

Preheat oven to 400°. Lightly grease a 9 x 13" baking dish with nonstick cooking spray; set aside.

In a large bowl, combine spaghetti sauce, ricotta cheese, broth, 1 cup mozzarella cheese and half the Parmesan cheese. Add uncooked pasta and meatballs; toss with sauce mixture until coated. Spread mixture in prepared baking dish. Cover tightly with aluminum foil and bake for 1 hour or until pasta is tender and meatballs are heated through. Remove from oven and sprinkle evenly with remaining 1 cup mozzarella cheese and remaining Parmesan cheese. Return to oven to bake uncovered 10 minutes longer or until cheese is melted and bubbling.

Beef

Hearty Beef Stew

serves 5

Ingredients

¼ C. flour
2 lbs. cubed stewing beef
2 T. vegetable oil
3 medium potatoes
1 (14.5 oz.) can stewed
   tomatoes with juice

1 (16 oz.) pkg. baby carrots
1 C. frozen green beans or corn
1 (1 oz.) pkg. dry onion soup mix
1 tsp. salt
¼ tsp. pepper

Preparation

Preheat oven to 400°. Pour flour into a large resealable plastic bag. Add meat, seal bag and shake well to coat. Spread vegetable oil in the bottom of a large roasting pan. Remove meat from bag and arrange in a single layer in pan. Bake for 30 minutes.

Meanwhile, peel and cut potatoes into chunks. Remove pan from oven and add 1½ cups water, potatoes, tomatoes, carrots, green beans, soup mix, salt and pepper. Stir well.

Reduce oven temperature to 375°. Cover pan and return to oven to bake 1½ to 2 hours longer or until meat reaches desired tenderness. Add more water partway through cooking time as needed.

Variation *Substitute frozen peas for green beans, but do not add to stew until the last ½ hour of cooking time.*

Dinner in the Bag

serves 8

Ingredients

½ C. flour

1 large oven cooking bag (16 x 17½")

1 (8 oz.) can tomato sauce

1 tsp. instant beef bouillon granules

½ tsp. salt

¼ tsp. pepper

1 (4 lb.) boneless rump roast

3 medium carrots, peeled

2 onions

3 celery stalks

1 red or green bell pepper, cored and seeded

8 whole new potatoes

Preparation

Preheat oven to 350°. Pour flour into oven bag and shake well. Place bag in a 9 x 13" baking pan (2" deep). Roll down top of bag and add tomato sauce, ½ cup water, dry bouillon, salt and pepper. Squeeze bag gently to mix. Place roast in bag. Quarter carrots and onions. Cut celery and bell pepper into 1" pieces. Add cut vegetables and whole potatoes to bag. Turn bag gently to coat ingredients with sauce. Close bag with nylon tie. With a sharp knife or scissors, cut six ½" slits in top of bag to let steam escape. Tuck ends of bag into pan. Place pan in oven and bake for 1¾ to 2¼ hours or until meat is fork-tender. Let stand 10 minutes.

With scissors, cut open the top of bag and carefully remove food; stir remaining juices in bag to blend. To serve, spoon juices over roast and vegetables.

Hash Brown Meatball Bake

serves 8

Ingredients

1 (24 oz.) pkg. frozen shredded
   hash brown potatoes, thawed*
1 C. sour cream, or less to taste
1 (10.75 oz.) can cream of potato
   or cream of chicken soup
¾ to 1 C. milk

2 tsp. dried chives
2 C. shredded colby
   cheese, divided
1½ C. frozen peas, optional
12 oz. frozen, fully cooked mini
   meatballs (about 24)

Preparation

Preheat oven to 350°. Lightly grease a 9 x 13" baking dish with
nonstick cooking spray. In prepared dish, combine potatoes,
sour cream, soup, milk, chives and 1½ cups cheese; mix until well
blended. Stir in peas, if desired, and spread evenly in dish. Top with
frozen meatballs. Cover dish tightly with aluminum foil and bake
for 40 minutes. Uncover and bake 25 to 35 minutes longer or until
bubbly and meatballs are crisp on top. Sprinkle with remaining
½ cup cheese and bake about 5 minutes longer to melt cheese.

* Thaw hash browns overnight in the refrigerator.

Potato-Topped Chili Loaf

serves 6

Ingredients

¾ C. diced onion
⅓ C. saltine cracker crumbs
1 egg
3 T. milk
1 T. chili powder
½ tsp. salt
¼ tsp. garlic powder, optional
1½ lbs. lean ground beef

3 C. hot mashed potatoes*
1 (11 oz.) can Mexicorn, drained
1 (15.5 oz.) can chili beans, drained
¼ C. thinly sliced green onions
¼ tsp. seasoned salt
1 C. shredded Cheddar or taco cheese, divided

Preparation

Preheat oven to 375°. In a large bowl, combine onion, cracker crumbs, egg, milk, chili powder, salt and garlic powder, if desired. Crumble uncooked ground beef over onion mixture and mix until well combined. Press meat mixture into an ungreased 9" square baking pan. Bake for 25 minutes or until no longer pink; drain.

Meanwhile, in a separate bowl, stir together potatoes, Mexicorn, chili beans, green onions, seasoned salt and ½ cup cheese; spread mixture over partially cooked meatloaf. Sprinkle remaining ½ cup cheese on top. Bake 15 minutes longer or until potato layer is lightly browned and heated through.

*Reheat leftover mashed potatoes, prepare instant mashed potatoes according to package directions or use frozen or refrigerated heat-and-serve microwavable mashed potatoes.

Presto Ground Beef & Noodles

serves 10

Ingredients

2 lbs. lean ground beef
Salt and pepper to taste
8 oz. uncooked egg noodles
1 C. chopped carrots
½ C. finely chopped onion
2 tsp. minced garlic
½ C. diced celery

1 (10.75 oz.) can cream of
  mushroom soup
1 (10.75 oz.) can chicken
  vegetable soup
¼ tsp. cayenne pepper
2 C. crushed potato chips

Preparation

Preheat oven to 350°. Grease a 9 x 13" baking dish with nonstick cooking spray. Crumble uncooked ground beef evenly over bottom of prepared dish; season with salt and pepper as desired. In layers, add uncooked noodles, carrots, onion, garlic and celery; set aside.

In a medium bowl, mix both soups, 1½ soup cans water and cayenne pepper until blended. Pour soup mixture over ingredients in dish. Cover and bake for 50 minutes or until meat is fully cooked and vegetables and noodles are tender. Remove from oven and sprinkle crushed potato chips over top; bake uncovered 10 minutes longer. Let stand 10 minutes before serving.

Beef

Autumn Harvest Beef

serves 4

Ingredients

2 lbs. butternut squash, peeled and seeded
4 medium potatoes, peeled
1 lb. stewing beef, trimmed
6 medium carrots, peeled
1 onion

2 tsp. instant beef bouillon granules
1 (8 oz.) can tomato sauce
½ tsp. sugar
½ tsp. salt
⅛ tsp. pepper

Preparation

Preheat oven to 300°. Cut squash, potatoes and beef into 1" cubes. Slice carrots and chop onion. In an ungreased 4-quart baking dish or medium roasting pan, layer squash, potatoes, carrots, beef and onion. Set aside.

In a medium bowl, combine ½ cup very hot water and dry bouillon; stir until dissolved. Stir in tomato sauce, sugar, salt and pepper until blended. Pour mixture over ingredients in baking dish. Cover and bake for 3½ to 4 hours or until beef and vegetables are tender.

Beef

Mexicali Mini Meatloaves

serves 4

Ingredients

1 (14.5 oz.) can stewed tomatoes with juice

1½ C. uncooked instant white rice

1 C. spicy tomato juice

½ C. diced red and/or green bell pepper

½ tsp. ground oregano

½ tsp. dry mustard

½ to 1 diced jalapeño pepper

2 T. dried minced onion, divided

1½ tsp. chili powder, divided

1 tsp. salt, divided

1 lb. lean ground beef

½ C. quick-cooking rolled oats

1 egg, lightly beaten

1 (8 oz.) can tomato sauce, divided

1 (4 oz.) can diced green chiles, divided

⅛ tsp. garlic powder

½ C. shredded Cheddar cheese

Preparation

Preheat oven to 350°. Grease an 8" square baking dish with nonstick cooking spray; set aside. Pour tomatoes into a large bowl; chop well. Stir in uncooked rice, tomato juice, bell pepper, oregano, dry mustard, jalapeño pepper, 2 teaspoons onion, ½ teaspoon chili powder and ½ teaspoon salt. Spread mixture in prepared dish and set aside.

In same large bowl, combine ground beef, oats, egg, ¼ cup tomato sauce, 2 tablespoons chiles, 1 tablespoon onion, remaining 1 teaspoon chili powder and ½ teaspoon salt; mix well. Shape into four 2x4" loaves and place on rice in dish. Cover with aluminum foil and bake for 50 minutes or until rice is tender.

In a small bowl, mix remaining tomato sauce, green chiles, 1 teaspoon onion and garlic powder. Spoon sauce over meatloaves and top with cheese. Return to oven for 10 minutes to melt cheese.

Speedy Reuben Hot Dish

serves 6

Ingredients

6 slices rye bread
1 lb. deli sliced corned beef
1 (14 oz.) can sauerkraut, drained

¾ to 1 C. Thousand Island or Russian salad dressing
2 C. shredded Swiss cheese

Preparation

Cut bread into cubes and spread evenly in the bottom of an ungreased 9 x 13" baking dish; put dish into cold oven. Set oven temperature to 400° and toast bread cubes for 5 to 10 minutes.

Remove dish from oven and spread sauerkraut evenly over bread cubes. Cut beef into strips and layer them over sauerkraut. Drizzle dressing over the top. Cover dish with aluminum foil that has been sprayed with nonstick cooking spray. Bake for 20 minutes. Remove foil, sprinkle cheese over top and bake uncovered 10 minutes longer, until cheese is melted and hot dish is bubbly.

Beef

Easy Minute Steak Bake

serves 4

Ingredients

4 tenderized minute steaks*
5 to 6 medium potatoes, peeled
5 to 6 medium carrots, peeled

1 (10.75 oz.) can cream of
mushroom soup

Preparation

Preheat oven to 375°. Grease a 9 x 13" baking dish with nonstick cooking spray. Place minute steaks in prepared dish. Thinly slice potatoes and carrots and arrange over meat. Spread soup over all. Cover dish tightly with aluminum foil and bake for 40 to 50 minutes or until meat is cooked through and vegetables are tender.

* You may also use tenderized round steak.

Beef

Overnight Meatball Casserole

serves 8

Ingredients

15 oz. pizza sauce (1¾ C.)
1 (10.75 oz.) can Cheddar cheese soup
½ C. chopped celery
1 T. minced garlic
½ C. chopped sweet onion
3 C. uncooked wide egg noodles or mini lasagna noodles (such as mafalda)

1 C. frozen stir-fry bell pepper and onion
1 (18 oz.) pkg. frozen, fully cooked Italian meatballs
1½ C. shredded mozzarella cheese
2 T. chopped fresh parsley

Preparation

In an ungreased 9 x 13" baking dish, combine pizza sauce, soup, 1 cup water, celery, garlic and onion; mix well. Stir in uncooked noodles and stir-fry vegetables. Add meatballs and toss to coat in sauce. If necessary for even coating, add more water, a little at a time. Cover dish tightly with aluminum foil and refrigerate at least 8 hours.

When ready to bake, preheat oven to 350°. Bake covered for 45 to 50 minutes. Remove dish from oven and sprinkle with cheese and parsley. Return to oven and bake uncovered 5 to 10 minutes longer or until cheese is melted and casserole is bubbly.

Hamburger Shepherd's Pie

serves 6

Ingredients

¼ C. fine dry bread crumbs
½ C. milk
1 egg
1 lb. lean ground beef
1 tsp. salt

¼ tsp. pepper
1 T. dried, minced onion
3 C. prepared mashed potatoes*
¾ C. shredded Cheddar cheese
Paprika

Preparation

Preheat oven to 350°. In a large bowl, combine bread crumbs and milk; let soak for several minutes. Stir in egg. Add uncooked ground beef, salt, pepper and onion; mix well. Lightly pat meat mixture into an ungreased 9" pie plate. Bake uncovered for 35 minutes.

Remove from oven and drain off fat. Spread mashed potatoes over the meat; sprinkle with cheese and paprika. Return to oven for 10 minutes more or until cheese is melted and potatoes are heated through.

Reheat leftover mashed potatoes, prepare instant mashed potatoes according to package directions or use frozen or refrigerated heat-and-serve microwavable mashed potatoes.

Cabbage-Rice Casserole

serves 4

Ingredients

½ head green cabbage
4 green onions
¾ lb. lean ground beef
¼ C. uncooked white rice

1 (10.75 oz.) can tomato soup
¼ tsp. garlic powder
Salt and pepper to taste

Preparation

Preheat oven to 350°. Grease a 2½-quart casserole dish with nonstick cooking spray. Slice cabbage or chop into small chunks; place in prepared dish. Slice green onions and sprinkle over cabbage. Cover with crumbled uncooked ground beef; set aside.

In a medium bowl, mix uncooked rice, soup, 1 soup can hot water and garlic powder. Season with salt and pepper as desired. Pour soup mixture over ingredients in dish. Cover tightly with aluminum foil and bake for 1 hour. Let stand 5 minutes before serving.

Swiss Steak & Baked Potatoes

serves 8

Ingredients

2 lbs. boneless round steak (½" thick)
¼ tsp. pepper
½ tsp. garlic powder
6 green onions
2 large carrots, peeled
1 celery stalk
1 (4 oz.) can sliced mushrooms, drained

1 (8 oz.) can tomato sauce
1 (14.5 oz.) can diced or stewed tomatoes with juice
1 T. Worcestershire sauce
8 baking potatoes
Olive oil
Coarse salt
Butter and/or sour cream, optional

Preparation

Preheat oven to 325°. Grease a 9 x 13" baking dish with nonstick cooking spray and set aside.

Trim fat from beef; tenderize as desired. Cut into serving-size pieces and place in prepared baking dish. Sprinkle with pepper and garlic powder. Slice green onions, carrots and celery, and place in a medium bowl. Add mushrooms, tomato sauce, tomatoes and Worcestershire sauce, stirring to blend. Pour vegetable mixture over meat to cover. Cover dish tightly with aluminum foil and begin baking meat on middle oven rack, setting timer for 45 minutes.

Meanwhile, scrub potatoes and pierce skins with a fork several times. After 45 minutes, rub potatoes with olive oil and roll in coarse salt. Set potatoes directly on upper oven rack to bake with the steak for another 1 to 1½ hours or until meat and potatoes are tender. Serve butter and sour cream with potatoes, if desired.

Meal-in-One Meatloaf

serves 4

Ingredients

4 baking potatoes
1 green bell pepper, cored and seeded
1 red bell pepper, cored and seeded
1 onion
2 T. vegetable oil
1 egg, lightly beaten

1 lb. lean ground beef
¼ C. minced fresh parsley
1 T. Worcestershire sauce
1 tsp. minced garlic
½ C. fine dry bread crumbs
2 zucchini
1 (8 oz.) can tomato sauce
Salt and pepper to taste

Preparation

Preheat oven to 400°. Grease a large roasting pan with nonstick cooking spray; set aside.

Peel potatoes, if desired. Thinly slice potatoes, both bell peppers and onion; place in prepared roasting pan, drizzle with vegetable oil and toss to coat. Bake uncovered for 20 minutes.

Meanwhile, in a large bowl, combine egg, ground beef, parsley, Worcestershire sauce, garlic and bread crumbs; mix thoroughly. Shape meat mixture into a 4 x 8" loaf.

When vegetables have baked for 20 minutes, remove pan from oven and reduce heat to 350°. Thinly slice zucchini and stir into vegetables in pan. Push vegetables to the sides of pan and place meat loaf in the center. Pour tomato sauce over meat and vegetables. Season with salt and pepper. Bake uncovered for 30 to 40 minutes or until vegetables are tender and meatloaf is fully cooked. Let stand several minutes before slicing.

Cut veggies beforehand and store in an airtight container until needed.

Beef

Pineapple Salsa Cube Steaks

serves 4

Ingredients

3 large potatoes, peeled

1 (15 oz.) can black beans, drained

4 tenderized cube or minute steaks

½ tsp. ground cumin

Salt and pepper to taste

1 green or red bell pepper, cored and seeded

1 onion

1 (16 oz.) jar peach-pineapple or pineapple salsa

1 C. shredded Monterey Jack cheese, divided

Preparation

Preheat oven to 375°. Grease a 9 x 13" baking dish with nonstick cooking spray. Thinly slice potatoes and place in bottom of prepared dish. Pour black beans over potatoes. Place steaks on beans and sprinkle with cumin, salt and pepper. Dice bell pepper and onion; sprinkle over meat. Pour salsa over all and sprinkle ½ cup cheese over top. Cover dish tightly with aluminum foil and bake for 40 minutes or until meat is cooked through. Uncover, sprinkle with remaining ½ cup cheese and return to oven to bake 10 minutes longer.

Variation *Use tomato salsa in place of the pineapple salsa and Mexican blend cheese in place of Monterey Jack cheese.*

Supper on a Bun

serves 6

Ingredients

½ C. milk
1½ lbs. lean ground beef
½ C. saltine cracker crumbs
1 egg, lightly beaten
½ C. chopped onion
1 T. prepared yellow mustard

1½ tsp. salt
⅛ tsp. pepper
2 C. shredded cheese, any type
1 loaf French bread, split
  lengthwise
Condiments as desired

Preparation

Preheat oven to 350°. In a large bowl, combine milk, uncooked ground beef, cracker crumbs, egg, onion, mustard, salt and pepper; mix well. Spread half of meat mixture on the cut side of each bread piece. Wrap aluminum foil around crust side of bread, leaving the meat uncovered. Place on a cookie sheet and bake for 25 minutes or until meat is fully cooked. Remove from oven, sprinkle cheese on top and return to oven for 5 minutes longer to melt cheese. Slice into pieces and serve with desired condiments.

Use just one section of French bread and cut recipe in half to serve 3 to 4 people.

Beef

Quick Pizza Hash

serves 3

Ingredients

1 (15 oz.) can corned
   beef hash, chilled
1 C. shredded cheese, any type
1 (8 oz.) can tomato sauce
1 (4 oz.) can sliced
   mushrooms, drained

½ tsp. garlic salt
½ tsp. dried oregano
2 T. grated Parmesan cheese

Preparation

Preheat oven to 375°. Remove hash from can in a solid log and cut crosswise into six even slices. Arrange slices in a 7 x 11" baking dish. Sprinkle shredded cheese over hash; set aside.

In a small bowl, mix tomato sauce, mushrooms, garlic salt and oregano; spoon over hash and cheese. Sprinkle with Parmesan cheese. Bake for 20 minutes or until cheese is melted and mixture is heated through.

Pork

Scalloped Potatoes & Ham

serves 6

Ingredients

1 (1 lb.) fully cooked ham slice, ½" thick

5 C. thinly sliced potatoes

1 (10.75 oz.) can cream of celery soup

¼ C. milk

½ C. finely chopped onion

¼ C. chopped green bell pepper

Dash of pepper

2 T. butter

1 C. shredded Cheddar cheese

Preparation

Preheat oven to 350°. Grease a shallow 2-quart casserole dish with nonstick cooking spray; set aside.

Cut ham into bite-size cubes. Place half the potatoes in prepared baking dish. Cover with ham pieces. Top with remaining potatoes and set aside.

In a medium bowl, combine soup, milk, onion, bell pepper and pepper; stir well. Pour mixture over potatoes and ham. Dot with butter. Cover dish with aluminum foil and bake for 1 hour or until potatoes are tender. Remove dish from oven and sprinkle cheese over potatoes. Return to oven to bake uncovered about 15 minutes longer to melt cheese.

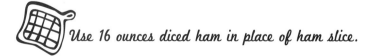 *Use 16 ounces diced ham in place of ham slice.*

Pork

Home-Baked Hot Pockets

serves 6

Ingredients

1 (13.8 oz.) tube refrigerated pizza crust

16 thin slices honey ham

6 slices salami

¼ C. ranch salad dressing, plus extra for dipping

1 C. shredded three cheese blend

6 tomato slices

Preparation

Preheat oven to 400°. Line a large cookie sheet with aluminum foil and lightly grease with nonstick cooking spray; set aside.

Unroll pizza dough on a lightly floured surface. Pat dough into a 12x18" rectangle; cut into six (4 x 9") rectangles. Top each dough rectangle with ham and salami, leaving ½" uncovered around edges and cutting ham to fit; set aside.

Spread about 2 teaspoons dressing over meat on each serving and sprinkle evenly with cheese. Top each with a tomato slice. Fold dough rectangles in half crosswise and seal cut edges together with a fork. Place on prepared cookie sheet and bake for 15 to 17 minutes or until golden brown.

Cheesy Mac & Smokies

serves 12

Ingredients

1 (16 oz.) pkg. uncooked elbow macaroni
2 T. melted butter
8 oz. shredded American cheese
8 oz. cubed Velveeta cheese
2 (12 oz.) cans evaporated milk
2 C. chicken broth or water
1 T. dried minced onion

4 eggs
2 tsp. dry mustard
1 tsp. salt
½ tsp. ground white pepper
¼ tsp. cayenne pepper
1 to 2 dashes of hot pepper sauce, optional
½ lb. sliced cocktail wieners or diced ham

Preparation

Preheat oven to 350°. In a deep 3-quart baking dish, toss together uncooked macaroni and melted butter until coated. Add American and Velveeta cheeses; stir lightly to combine and set aside.

In a medium bowl, whisk together evaporated milk, broth, onion, eggs, dry mustard, salt, white pepper, cayenne pepper and hot pepper sauce, if desired. Pour over macaroni mixture and stir in wieners until well combined. Bake uncovered for 45 to 55 minutes or until center is set and macaroni is tender, stirring once halfway through cooking time. Remove from oven and let stand 5 minutes before serving.

For a crunchy top, sprinkle casserole with buttered bread crumbs halfway through cooking time.

Oktoberfest Pork Chop Combo

serves 4

Ingredients

1 large unpeeled apple
1 (14 oz.) can sauerkraut, drained
4 pork chops (¾" thick)
Seasoned salt to taste
Paprika
1 C. uncooked instant couscous

½ tsp. salt
1½ C. boiling chicken stock
1 T. olive oil
¼ tsp. garlic powder
¼ C. thinly sliced green
 onions, optional

Preparation

Preheat oven to 350°. Lightly grease a 7 x 11" baking dish with nonstick cooking spray; set aside.

Coarsely grate the apple into a medium bowl. Stir in sauerkraut. Spread mixture in the bottom of prepared baking dish. Arrange pork chops over sauerkraut mixture. Sprinkle chops with seasoned salt and paprika. Cover dish tightly with aluminum foil and bake for 50 to 60 minutes or until pork is fully cooked. If desired, uncover during last 10 minutes of baking for browning. Let stand at least 3 minutes before serving.

About 10 minutes before pork chops are done, make couscous. Place uncooked couscous and salt in a medium bowl. Add boiling chicken stock and olive oil; stir just to blend. Immediately cover bowl tightly with aluminum foil and let stand 5 minutes. Uncover and fluff with a fork; stir in garlic powder and green onions, if desired. Serve alongside pork chop combo.

Pork

Honey Mustard Kielbasa

serves 6

Ingredients

¾ C. chicken broth
    or amber beer
¼ C. honey mustard
2 T. brown sugar

1 (14 oz.) pkg. kielbasa
1¼ lbs. red potatoes
1 onion

Preparation

Preheat oven to 400°. In a small bowl, whisk together broth, honey mustard and brown sugar until blended. Slice kielbasa into 1" pieces and place in an ungreased 2-quart shallow baking dish. Cut potatoes into ¾" cubes and slice onion; layer over kielbasa. Drizzle broth mixture over all and toss to coat well. Cover dish tightly with aluminum foil and bake for 55 minutes or until potatoes are tender, stirring several times during cooking.

Baked Sausage Ravioli

serves 6

Ingredients

1 (25 oz.) pkg. frozen Italian-style, sausage-filled ravioli, thawed

1 (4 oz.) can sliced mushrooms, drained

1 C. sliced zucchini, optional

½ C. pepperoni slices

1 (26 oz.) jar roasted tomato and garlic pasta sauce

1 C. shredded Swiss cheese

⅛ tsp. dried Italian seasoning

1 tsp. dried basil, optional

Preparation

Preheat oven to 350°. In a large bowl, mix ravioli, mushrooms, zucchini, pepperoni and pasta sauce. Spoon into an ungreased 8" square baking dish or 2-quart casserole dish. Sprinkle with cheese, Italian seasoning and basil, if desired. Bake for 40 to 50 minutes or until heated through and bubbly.

Variation *Make it meatless by using cheese-filled ravioli.*

Hash Brown & Ham Bake

serves 10

Ingredients

1 (16 oz.) container sour cream

1 (10.75 oz.) can cream of chicken soup

1 (30 oz.) pkg. frozen diced hash brown potatoes

2 C. fully cooked diced ham

2 C. cubed American cheese (8 oz.)

¼ C. chopped onion

2 C. crushed corn flakes cereal

½ C. melted butter

1 C. shredded mozzarella cheese

Preparation

Preheat oven to 350°. In a large bowl, mix sour cream and soup. Stir in frozen potatoes, ham, American cheese and onion until well blended. Pour mixture into an ungreased 9 x 13" baking dish and spread evenly; set aside.

In a medium bowl, stir together corn flakes and butter until coated. Sprinkle cereal mixture over ingredients in dish. Bake uncovered for 30 minutes. Remove from oven and sprinkle with mozzarella cheese. Return to oven and bake 20 to 25 minutes longer or until heated through and bubbly around edges.

Chops & Corn Stuffing

serves 4

Ingredients

1½ C. cornbread stuffing mix
1 (10.75 oz.) can cream
of celery soup
½ C. whole kernel corn
½ C. finely chopped onion

¼ C. finely chopped celery
4 boneless pork chops (1" thick)
1 T. brown sugar
1 tsp. Dijon mustard

Preparation

Preheat oven to 400°. Grease a 9" deep-dish pie plate with nonstick cooking spray; set aside.

In a medium bowl, combine dry stuffing mix, soup, corn, onion and celery; mix well. Spoon stuffing mixture into prepared pie plate. Arrange pork chops on top and set aside.

In a small bowl, mix brown sugar and Dijon mustard until smooth. Spread mustard mixture on pork chops. Bake uncovered for 35 minutes or until pork is fully cooked. Let stand at least 3 minutes before serving.

Classic Beanie-Weinies

serves 8

Ingredients

2 (15 oz.) cans pork and beans in tomato sauce
1 (1 oz.) env. dry onion soup mix
⅓ C. ketchup

2 T. brown sugar
1 T. prepared yellow mustard
1 (16 oz.) pkg. frankfurters (classic or turkey)

Preparation

Preheat oven to 350°. In an ungreased 2-quart casserole dish, combine pork and beans, soup mix, ¼ cup water, ketchup, brown sugar and mustard. Stir until well mixed. Cut franks crosswise into ½" slices. Add to dish and stir thoroughly. Bake uncovered for 1 hour.

Deli Delight

Ingredients

2 (8 oz.) tubes refrigerated
   crescent rolls*
¼ lb. thinly sliced deli ham
¼ lb. thinly sliced
   provolone cheese
¼ lb. thinly sliced Swiss cheese
¼ lb. thinly sliced Genoa salami

¼ lb. thinly sliced pepperoni
1 (12 oz.) jar roasted
   red peppers, drained
3 eggs, lightly beaten
3 T. grated Parmesan cheese
½ tsp. pepper
½ tsp. garlic powder

Preparation

Preheat oven to 375°. Unroll one tube of crescent roll dough and cover the bottom of a 9 x 13" baking dish, pressing perforations together. Pat ham dry with paper towels. Layer ham over crust followed by provolone and Swiss cheeses, salami and pepperoni. Cut red peppers into thin strips and pat dry with paper towels. Arrange over pepperoni; set aside.

In a small bowl, combine eggs, Parmesan cheese, pepper and garlic powder. Pour about ⅔ of egg mixture over ingredients in dish. Unroll second tube of crescent rolls and place dough over peppers as a top crust. Brush crust with remaining egg mixture. Cover with aluminum foil and bake for 25 minutes. Remove foil and bake 15 to 20 minutes more or until dough is golden brown. Let stand at least 15 minutes before cutting into squares. Serve warm or at room temperature.

* You may also use seamless cresent dough sheets.

Baked Dirty Rice

serves 6

Ingredients

1 C. uncooked instant white rice

1 lb. ground bulk sausage

1 (10.75 oz.) can cream of celery soup

1 (10.75 oz.) can French onion soup

1 tsp. browning and seasoning sauce (such as Kitchen Bouquet)

½ C. chopped green bell pepper

½ C. chopped celery

½ C. chopped green onion

1 tsp. salt

¼ to ½ tsp. cayenne pepper, or to taste

Cajun seasoning, optional

Preparation

Preheat oven to 425°. Lightly grease a 2-quart casserole dish and set aside.

In a large bowl, combine uncooked rice, crumbled uncooked sausage, both cans of soup, browning sauce, bell pepper, celery, green onion, salt, cayenne pepper and Cajun seasoning to taste, if desired; mix well. Spoon into prepared casserole dish and cover tightly with aluminum foil. Bake for 1 hour or until meat is thoroughly cooked and rice is tender.

Pork

Sweet & Savory Pork Loin

serves 14

Ingredients

1 tsp. dried sage
1 tsp. dried thyme
1 tsp. dried rosemary
1 tsp. dried marjoram
Salt and pepper to taste
1 red onion

3 celery stalks
1 (4 to 6 lb.) pork loin roast
4 tart apples, peeled, cored
3 yams, peeled
3 T. brown sugar
1 C. apple juice

Preparation

In a small bowl, mix sage, thyme, rosemary, marjoram, salt and pepper. Rub over roast. Cover roast and refrigerate overnight.

When ready to bake, preheat oven to 325°. Chop onion and celery; place in the bottom of a large roasting pan. Set roast on top of vegetables, cover and bake for 1 hour.

Meanwhile, chop apples and place in a medium bowl. Slice yams and add to bowl. Sprinkle with brown sugar and stir to coat. Remove pan from oven after 1 hour and arrange apples and yams around roast. Pour apple juice over all. Cover pan and return to oven for about 1½ hours longer or until meat is tender and fully cooked. Baste with juice partway through baking time.

You may also rub roast with seasonings in the morning and refrigerate for just 6 hours before baking. It will be ready for your evening meal.

Broccoli-Ham Casserole

serves 6

Ingredients

1 (10 to 12 oz.) pkg. frozen chopped broccoli
2 C. uncooked instant white rice
½ C. chopped onion
1 (15 oz.) jar Cheez Whiz
1 (10.75 oz.) can cream of chicken soup

¾ C. milk
1½ to 2 C. fully cooked diced ham
2 C. croutons

Preparation

Preheat oven to 350°. Lightly grease an 8" square baking dish with nonstick cooking spray. Place broccoli, uncooked rice and onion in prepared dish; mix well and set aside.

In a blender container, combine Cheese Whiz, soup and milk; blend until smooth. Pour half of cheese mixture over rice mixture in baking dish; cover with ham. Pour remaining cheese mixture over ham. Top with croutons. Bake uncovered for 45 minutes.

Easy Crust Pizza Bake

serves 6

Ingredients

3⅓ C. biscuit baking mix
1 C. milk
1 (15 oz.) can pizza
   sauce, divided
8 oz. sliced pepperoni, divided

Choice of other toppings (sliced
   olives, bell peppers, onions,
   mushrooms, Canadian bacon
   or cooked sausage)
2 C. shredded mozzarella
   cheese, divided

Preparation

Preheat oven to 375°. Grease a 9 x 13" baking dish with nonstick
cooking spray; set aside.

In a medium bowl, combine baking mix and milk; stir until a soft
dough forms. Drop half of dough by spoonfuls evenly over bottom
of prepared baking dish (dough will not completely cover bottom
of dish). Drizzle half the pizza sauce over dough. Scatter half the
pepperoni over the sauce. Add other toppings as desired. Top with
1 cup cheese. Repeat layers with remaining dough, sauce, pepperoni,
other toppings and cheese. Bake for 20 to 25 minutes or until
golden brown.

Pork

Wild Rice & Pork Chop Delight

serves 4

Ingredients

⅔ C. uncooked wild rice
1 (14.5 oz.) can chicken broth
¼ C. apple cider or white wine
1 C. chopped onion

4 pork chops (1" thick)
1 tart apple, cored
1 medium tomato
Chopped fresh parsley

Preparation

Preheat oven to 325°. Lightly grease a 2-quart casserole dish with nonstick cooking spray. Rinse rice well and place in prepared dish. Add broth, cider and onion; stir to mix. Arrange pork chops over rice. Cover dish tightly with aluminum foil and bake for 1 hour.

Meanwhile, slice apple and tomato into four slices. After 1 hour, remove casserole dish from oven and top each chop with one apple slice and one tomato slice. Cover and return to oven to bake 30 minutes longer.

Taste of Autumn Chops

serves 6

Ingredients

1 (6 oz.) pkg. stuffing mix
  for pork or chicken
Water and butter as listed
  on stuffing package
1 (21 oz.) can apple pie filling

1 tsp. ground cinnamon,
  optional
6 boneless pork chops (¾" thick)
Salt and pepper to taste

Preparation

Preheat oven to 375°. Grease a 9 x 13" baking dish with nonstick cooking spray; set aside.

Combine stuffing mix with hot water and butter as listed on package; set aside. Spread pie filling over the bottom of prepared baking dish. Sprinkle with cinnamon, if desired. Arrange pork chops over apples and season with salt and pepper. Spoon warm stuffing mixture over chops. Cover dish tightly with aluminum foil and bake for 30 minutes. Uncover and bake 10 minutes longer or until pork chops are fully cooked. Cover loosely and let stand about 5 minutes before serving.

Pork

Ham Balls & Rice

serves 12

Ingredients

1¼ lbs. ground ham
1 lb. ground pork
½ lb. lean ground beef
1½ C. graham cracker crumbs
2 eggs, lightly beaten
1 C. milk
1 (10.75 oz.) can tomato soup

6 T. white vinegar
1¼ C. brown sugar
1 tsp. dry mustard
3 C. uncooked brown rice
2 tsp. salt
2 T. butter
5 C. boiling water

Preparation

Preheat oven to 350°. Grease two 9 x 13" baking dishes with nonstick cooking spray and set aside.

In a large bowl, combine ground ham, pork and beef with cracker crumbs, eggs and milk; mix well. Wet hands and shape meat mixture into 24 to 30 balls. Place ham balls in one prepared baking dish. In a small bowl, whisk together tomato soup, vinegar, brown sugar and dry mustard. Pour sauce mixture over meatballs. Cover dish with aluminum foil and set aside.

Place uncooked rice, salt and butter in second prepared dish. Pour boiling water over rice mixture and stir until butter melts. Cover dish tightly with aluminum foil. Place rice dish on upper rack in oven and meatballs on lower rack. Bake for 1 hour or until rice is tender and meatballs are fully cooked. Fluff rice with a fork before serving alongside meatballs.

One-Hour Chops & Sweet Potatoes

serves 6

Ingredients

6 medium sweet potatoes
6 pork chops (¾" thick)
¼ C. melted butter
1 C. finely crushed saltine
   crackers

¼ tsp. pepper
¼ to ½ tsp. ground sage
¼ to ½ tsp. dried thyme
Butter, cinnamon/sugar
   mixture, optional

Preparation

Preheat oven to 325°. Pierce sweet potato skins several times with a fork. Wrap each sweet potato in aluminum foil and immediately place on upper rack in oven to begin baking.

Meanwhile, pat pork chops dry with paper towels. In a small bowl, combine melted butter, cracker crumbs, pepper, sage and thyme; mix well. Coat chops thoroughly with crumb mixture, using hands as needed to press mixture on chops. Arrange chops in a single layer on a rack in a shallow baking pan with sides. Place uncovered pan on lower rack in oven and bake chops and potatoes for 1 hour, without turning, until cooked through and tender.

Remove pork chops and sweet potatoes from oven and let stand about 5 minutes before serving. Serve butter and sugar/cinnamon with potatoes, if desired.

Tropical Pork Kabobs

serves 6

Ingredients

2 lbs. boneless pork tenderloin roast

½ C. plus 1 T. pineapple juice, divided

1 T. lemon juice

¼ tsp. garlic powder

1 green bell pepper, cored and seeded

1 sweet onion

15 to 20 fresh mushrooms

18 pineapple chunks

½ C. apricot preserves

½ C. brown sugar

2 T. melted butter

¼ tsp. ground cloves

1½ C. uncooked white rice

1 tsp. salt

1 T. butter

3 C. boiling water

Preparation

Cut pork into 1" cubes; place in a large resealable plastic bag. Add ½ cup pineapple juice, lemon juice and garlic powder, seal bag and shake; marinate for 30 minutes. Cut bell pepper and onion into 1" pieces; set aside. Line a jelly roll pan with aluminum foil; oil lightly and set aside.

When ready to bake, preheat oven to 375°. Remove pork from bag and discard marinade. On 10 to 12 metal or soaked wooden skewers, alternately thread pieces of pork, bell pepper, onion, mushrooms and pineapple. Place skewers in prepared pan. In a small bowl, mix preserves, brown sugar, melted butter, remaining 1 tablespoon pineapple juice and cloves. Spoon half of sauce over kabobs; reserve remaining sauce.

Grease a 2-quart casserole dish with nonstick cooking spray. Place uncooked rice, salt and butter in prepared dish. Pour boiling water over rice and stir until butter melts. Cover dish tightly with aluminum foil and place on upper rack in oven; place kabobs on lower rack. Bake for 30 minutes or until rice is tender and meat is thoroughly cooked. Turn kabobs after 15 minutes and baste several times with reserved sauce. Fluff rice with a fork before serving with kabobs.

Poultry

Roasted Whole Chicken

serves 6

Ingredients

1 tsp. salt
2 tsp. sugar
¼ tsp. ground cloves
¼ tsp. ground allspice
¼ tsp. ground nutmeg
¼ tsp. ground cinnamon
1 (4 to 5 lb.) whole chicken

½ onion
5 cloves garlic, peeled
2 lbs. potatoes (4 large)
3 T. olive oil
Dried parsley or rosemary
Salt and pepper to taste
1 pt. cherry tomatoes

Preparation

Preheat oven to 400°. In a bowl, mix 1 teaspoon salt, sugar, cloves, allspice, nutmeg and cinnamon. Rub part of spice mixture underneath the skin of chicken; rub remaining mixture over skin. Thickly slice onion and crush garlic cloves; stuff into chicken cavity. Set chicken, breast side down, on a rack in a large foil-lined roasting pan. Roast chicken uncovered for 30 minutes.

Reduce oven temperature to 350°. Cut potatoes into 1" pieces (if using new potatoes, leave whole). In a bowl, toss potatoes with olive oil to coat; season with parsley, salt and pepper as desired. Arrange potatoes around chicken and roast for 1¼ to 1½ hours longer, stirring once, until chicken is cooked through and potatoes are tender. Add tomatoes during the final 20 minutes of cooking time.

Variation *To potatoes, add chunks of carrot, celery and/or peeled yam and toss with oil; season and cook as directed. Add water to pan as needed.*

After applying rub, chicken may be refrigerated for up to 24 hours; then stuff and roast.

Honey of a Turkey Dinner

serves 8

Ingredients

1 (5 to 6 lb.) turkey breast
Olive oil
Salt and pepper to taste
5 large carrots, peeled
3 celery stalks
4 medium parsnips, peeled

2 large rutabagas, peeled
3 onions
¼ C. honey
¼ C. balsamic vinegar
1 tsp. lemon pepper seasoning
1 tsp. paprika

Preparation

Preheat oven to 325°. Place turkey breast, skin side up, in a shallow roasting pan. Brush lightly with olive oil and season with salt and pepper. Insert oven-proof meat thermometer in thickest part of breast, without touching bone. Roast turkey uncovered for 1¼ hours.

Meanwhile, in a small bowl, mix honey, balsamic vinegar, lemon pepper seasoning and paprika; set aside for later use. Slice carrots into sticks; cut celery, rutabagas and parsnips into 1" pieces. Thickly slice onions. Remove roasting pan from oven and arrange vegetables around turkey. Return pan to oven to cook for 30 minutes.

Brush turkey with some of honey mixture; drizzle remaining mixture over vegetables. Roast for 30 minutes more or until thermometer reaches 165°. Halfway through last 30 minutes, stir vegetables to glaze with pan juices. Let turkey stand 10 minutes before carving. Spoon juices over turkey slices or serve separately.

Variation *Substitute Yukon gold potatoes, turnips, carrots and/or frozen thawed artichoke hearts for vegetables listed.*

Taco Chicken Hoedown

serves 6

Ingredients

6 ears corn on the cob, in
husks, room temperature
⅔ C. flour
1 (1 oz.) env. taco seasoning mix
¼ tsp. salt

1 egg
1 T. milk
6 small boneless, skinless
chicken breast halves
Butter and salt, optional

Preparation

Preheat oven to 350°. Line a 9 x 13" baking dish with aluminum foil
and grease with nonstick cooking spray; set aside. Trim off exposed
silk from ears of corn. Set ears (in husks) on an ungreased jelly roll
pan and place on lower rack in oven to cook for 15 minutes.

Meanwhile, in a shallow bowl, combine flour, seasoning mix and salt.
In a small bowl, whisk together egg and milk. Dip chicken pieces
in egg mixture and then roll in flour mixture to coat well. Arrange
chicken in prepared baking dish and place uncovered dish on upper
rack in oven with corn. Bake both dishes for 30 to 35 minutes more
or until chicken is cooked through and corn is tender. Let corn stand
at least 5 minutes before peeling off husks and silk. Serve corn with
butter and salt as desired.

Variation *If fresh corn isn't available, slice butternut squash into six
pieces and place cut side down in a 9 x 13" baking dish with ½" water.
Cover with foil and bake with chicken.*

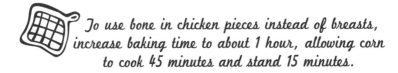
*To use bone in chicken pieces instead of breasts,
increase baking time to about 1 hour, allowing corn
to cook 45 minutes and stand 15 minutes.*

Turkey Enchilada Casserole

serves 6

Ingredients

1 C. milk
1 C. chopped cooked turkey*
1 C. tomato sauce
½ C. chopped onion
½ C. chopped green bell pepper
½ (4 oz.) can sliced mushrooms, drained
1 (4 oz.) can diced green chiles

1 tsp. chili powder
½ tsp. ground cumin
½ tsp. garlic salt
Pepper to taste
8 (6") corn tortillas
1 C. shredded Cheddar cheese
¼ C. chicken broth

Preparation

Preheat oven to 350°. Grease a 9 x 13" baking dish with nonstick cooking spray; set aside.

In a large bowl, combine milk, turkey, tomato sauce, onion, bell pepper, mushrooms, chiles, chili powder, cumin, garlic salt and pepper; mix well. Quarter all the tortillas and line prepared baking dish with half the tortilla pieces. Pour turkey mixture over tortillas and sprinkle with cheese. Arrange remaining tortillas over the top. Pour broth over all. Cover dish with aluminum foil and bake for 30 minutes. Let stand several minutes before serving.

You may substitute chopped cooked chicken or one 9.75-ounce can chunk chicken for the turkey.

Thai Chicken Pizza

serves 4

Ingredients

- 1 (12") ready-to-bake thin pizza crust
- 1 (6 oz.) pkg. frozen, fully cooked chicken breast strips
- ⅓ C. crunchy peanut butter
- ⅔ C. prepared peanut satay sauce
- ½ tsp. olive oil

- ¼ tsp. red pepper flakes, or to taste
- 2 C. shredded Monterey Jack cheese, divided
- ¼ C. finely shredded carrot
- ¼ C. thinly sliced green onion
- 2 T. chopped fresh cilantro

Preparation

Preheat oven to 450°. Place pizza crust on an ungreased pizza pan or cookie sheet; set aside.

Dice chicken strips into a medium bowl and set aside. In a small bowl, combine peanut butter, satay sauce, olive oil and red pepper flakes; stir to blend. Add ¼ cup peanut mixture to chicken and stir gently to coat. Spread remaining ¾ cup peanut mixture over pizza crust. Top with chicken mixture and 1½ cups cheese. Bake for 10 to 12 minutes or until cheese is bubbly and golden brown. Remove pizza from oven. Top with carrot, green onion, cilantro and remaining ½ cup cheese. Let stand until cheese melts; cut and serve.

Luscious Lemon Chicken

serves 4

Ingredients

1 (25 oz.) pkg. frozen steam-and-mash potatoes
4 bone-in chicken breast halves
2 T. olive oil
2 T. lemon juice

1 tsp. finely grated lemon zest
3 T. minced garlic
½ tsp. salt
½ tsp. pepper

Preparation

Preheat oven to 375°. Line a large jelly roll pan with aluminum foil; set aside.

Arrange frozen potatoes evenly on prepared pan. Place uncooked chicken pieces on top of potatoes. In a small bowl, whisk together olive oil, lemon juice, lemon zest and garlic; spoon evenly over chicken. Sprinkle with salt and pepper. Bake uncovered for 50 to 60 minutes or until chicken is cooked through and potatoes are lightly browned.

Chicken drumsticks and thighs may be used in place of breasts. Adjust cooking time as needed for doneness.

Poultry

One-Dish Chicken Bake

serves 6

Ingredients

1 (10.75 oz.) can cream of chicken, mushroom or celery soup

1 C. chicken broth or water

1 (6 oz.) pkg. long grain/wild rice mix with seasoning packet

1 (16 oz.) pkg. frozen vegetable combo (broccoli, carrots, water chestnuts)

1 C. shredded Cheddar cheese, divided

1 to 2 tsp. soy sauce, optional

6 boneless, skinless chicken breast halves

Paprika

Preparation

Preheat oven to 375°. In a 3-quart shallow baking dish, combine soup, broth, rice, seasoning mix, vegetables, ½ cup cheese and soy sauce, if desired; stir until well blended. Arrange uncooked chicken pieces on top of rice mixture and sprinkle with paprika. Cover dish tightly with aluminum foil and bake for 1 hour or until chicken is cooked through and juices run clear. Remove from oven and sprinkle remaining ½ cup cheese on top before serving.

Variation *Cut uncooked chicken tenderloin strips into bite-size pieces to use in place of whole chicken breast pieces, and substitute a box of broccoli au gratin-flavor Rice-a-Roni for the wild rice mix.*

Topsy-Turvy Pot Pie

serves 4

Ingredients

1 refrigerated pie crust

2 C. frozen, fully cooked chicken breast strips, thawed

1 C. frozen peas and carrots, slightly thawed

½ C. Alfredo pasta sauce

1 egg, lightly beaten

Preparation

Allow pie crust to stand at room temperature for 30 minutes. Unroll crust and place pastry circle on a large ungreased jelly roll pan; set aside. Preheat oven to 400°.

Dice chicken strips into a medium bowl. Add vegetables and pasta sauce; stir to blend. Spoon chicken mixture over the center of pastry circle, leaving a 3" border uncovered. Working in short sections around the entire pastry edge, fold border up and over the edge of filling, overlapping pastry to make pleats. Pinch the pleats well to contain the filling and create a round, open-topped pie. Brush pastry with egg. Bake for 30 minutes or until pastry is golden brown and filling is hot. Remove from oven and let pie stand 5 minutes before cutting into wedges to serve.

 This pot pie may also be made with leftover chopped cooked chicken or turkey.

Chicken & Veggie Bake

serves 4

Ingredients

4 boneless, skinless chicken breast halves
1 (1 oz.) env. dry onion soup mix
1½ C. buttermilk or sour milk*
1 T. flour
1 tsp. minced garlic

2 C. frozen mixed vegetables
¼ C. bread crumbs
Paprika
1 T. melted butter
Salt and pepper to taste

Preparation

Preheat oven to 350°. Pat chicken dry with paper towels. In a medium bowl, combine soup mix, buttermilk, flour and garlic; mix well and set aside. Lightly grease a large casserole dish with nonstick cooking spray. Arrange vegetables and uncooked chicken pieces in prepared dish. Pour buttermilk mixture over chicken. Cover dish tightly with aluminum foil and bake for 20 minutes.

Remove from oven and sprinkle bread crumbs and paprika over chicken. Drizzle with melted butter. Return to oven and bake uncovered for 25 minutes longer or until chicken is fully cooked. Season with salt and pepper before serving.

Make sour milk by mixing 1½ tablespoons lemon juice or vinegar with enough milk to make 1½ cups. Let stand 5 minutes before using.

Can-Can Chicken Casserole

serves 6

Ingredients

1 (12.5 oz.) can chunk white chicken, drained

1 (4 oz.) can sliced mushrooms, drained

1 (14 oz.) can mixed Chinese vegetables, drained

1 (8 oz.) can sliced water chestnuts, drained

1 (10.75 oz.) can cream of mushroom soup

1 (10.75 oz.) can cream of celery soup

1 (12 oz.) can evaporated milk

15 round butter crackers, optional

2 (5 oz.) cans chow mein noodles

Preparation

Preheat oven to 350°. Lightly grease a large casserole dish with nonstick cooking spray; set aside.

In a large bowl, break up chicken with a fork. Add mushrooms, Chinese vegetables, water chestnuts, both cans of soup and evaporated milk. Stir until well blended. Pour mixture into prepared casserole dish. If desired, crush crackers and sprinkle crumbs over the top. Bake uncovered for 40 to 45 minutes or until hot and bubbly. Serve over chow mein noodles.

Variation *Substitute one can cream of chicken soup and one can chicken and rice soup for the soups listed in recipe and add ¼ cup chopped onion. Omit chow mein noodles and serve baked mixture over cooked rice or Chinese noodles of choice.*

Poultry

Monterey Chicken Dinner

serves 4

Ingredients

4 boneless, skinless chicken breast halves

1 C. tomato salsa, divided

2 T. lime juice, divided

6 medium red potatoes

½ C. melted butter, divided

Salt and pepper to taste

1½ C. shredded Mexican cheese blend

¼ C. chopped fresh cilantro

8 lime wedges, optional

Preparation

Place chicken in a large resealable plastic bag. Add ½ cup salsa and 1 tablespoon lime juice. Seal bag and turn several times to coat chicken; marinate for 30 minutes.

When ready to bake, preheat oven to 425°. Line a 9 x 13" baking pan with aluminum foil and set aside. Cube potatoes and place in a medium bowl. Drizzle with 1 tablespoon melted butter and toss until coated. Arrange potatoes in a single layer in prepared pan. Season lightly with salt and pepper. Bake uncovered for 10 to 15 minutes.

Remove pan from oven and push potatoes to the sides of pan. Remove chicken from bag and discard marinade; arrange chicken in center of pan. Stir together remaining 3 tablespoons melted butter and 1 tablespoon lime juice; brush over chicken. Bake 20 to 30 minutes longer or until chicken is cooked through and juices run clear. Meanwhile, in a small bowl, toss together cheese, cilantro and remaining ½ cup salsa. Sprinkle over chicken and potatoes and bake a few minutes more to melt cheese. Serve with lime wedges, if desired.

Hot Chicken Salad

serves 6

Ingredients

2 (9.75 oz.) cans white chunk
   chicken, drained
2 C. diced celery
½ C. toasted sliced almonds*
½ tsp. salt

2 tsp. lemon juice
1 C. mayonnaise
1½ C. crushed potato chips
½ C. diced Velveeta cheese

Preparation

Preheat oven to 400°. Grease a 2-quart casserole dish with nonstick cooking spray; set aside.

In a medium bowl, break up chicken with a fork. Add celery, almonds, salt, lemon juice and mayonnaise; toss until well mixed. Transfer mixture to prepared casserole dish. Top with potato chips and cheese. Bake uncovered for 15 to 20 minutes or until heated through.

*To toast, place almonds in a single layer in a dry skillet over
   medium heat or on a baking sheet in a 350° oven for approximately
   10 minutes or until golden brown.*

You may also make this with 2 cups frozen, fully cooked chicken breast strips, thawed and diced.

Chicken Italiano

serves 4

Ingredients

6 oz. uncooked thin spaghetti
½ C. boiling water
⅔ C. multi-grain cracker crumbs
2 T. Parmesan cheese,
   plus more for topping
¼ tsp. garlic powder
1 tsp. dried Italian seasoning

2 T. milk
4 boneless, skinless chicken
   breast halves
2 C. garlic and herb
   pasta sauce, divided
1 C. shredded mozzarella
   cheese

Preparation

Preheat oven to 350°. Break spaghetti noodles in half or thirds and spread evenly in the bottom of an ungreased 7 x 11" baking dish. Pour boiling water over spaghetti, cover dish and let stand 10 minutes.

Meanwhile, in a shallow bowl, mix cracker crumbs, Parmesan cheese, garlic powder and Italian seasoning until blended. Pour milk into another bowl; dip chicken pieces in milk and then roll in cracker mixture to coat well. Set aside.

Pour 1⅓ cups pasta sauce over undrained spaghetti in baking dish and stir gently to separate pasta strands. Set coated chicken pieces on top of spaghetti and sauce. Cover dish tightly with aluminum foil and bake for 20 to 25 minutes or until chicken is almost cooked through. Remove dish from oven and pour part of remaining sauce over each chicken breast; stir the remaining sauce into exposed spaghetti. Sprinkle mozzarella cheese over chicken. Cover and return to oven for 5 to 10 minutes or until cheese is melted, chicken is fully cooked and spaghetti is tender. Let stand at least 5 minutes. Sprinkle with more Parmesan cheese before serving.

Cheesy Chicken-Broccoli Bake

serves 10

Ingredients

- 2 (9 oz.) pkgs. frozen, grilled chicken breast strips
- 2 C. uncooked instant rice
- 2 C. boiling water
- 1 (12 oz.) pkg. frozen broccoli florets, partially thawed
- 1½ C. frozen peas
- 1 (10.75 oz.) can cream of chicken soup
- 1 (10.75 oz.) can fiesta nacho cheese soup
- 1 (10 oz.) can diced tomatoes and green chiles with juice
- ½ C. milk
- ¼ to ½ tsp. red pepper flakes
- ½ C. shredded Cheddar cheese, divided
- ½ C. shredded mozzarella cheese, divided
- 1 C. crushed round butter crackers

Preparation

Preheat oven to 375°. Arrange chicken in an ungreased 9 x 13" baking dish. In a large bowl, combine uncooked rice and boiling water. Stir in broccoli and peas; spread mixture over chicken and set aside.

In a medium bowl, combine both cans of soup, tomatoes, milk and red pepper flakes. Stir in ¼ cup Cheddar cheese and ¼ cup mozzarella cheese; pour over broccoli mixture. Cover with aluminum foil and bake for 25 to 30 minutes. Remove from oven and top with crushed crackers, remaining ¼ cup Cheddar cheese and ¼ cup mozzarella cheese. Bake uncovered for 15 to 20 minutes longer or until vegetables and rice are tender and topping is golden brown.

 You may also use 3 cups leftover diced chicken, rotisserie chicken or canned chicken.

Phyllo Turkey Pie

serves 8

Ingredients

4 green onions
½ tsp. minced garlic
3 eggs, slightly beaten
1 (10 oz.) pkg. frozen chopped spinach, thawed and drained
1 C. shredded mozzarella cheese
⅔ C. milk

2 T. grated Parmesan cheese
¼ tsp. pepper
2 C. chopped cooked turkey or chicken*
3 T. melted butter
4 (14 x 18") sheets frozen phyllo dough, thawed

Preparation

Preheat oven to 375°. Thinly slice green onions into a large bowl. Add garlic, eggs, spinach, mozzarella cheese, milk, Parmesan cheese and pepper; mix well. Add turkey and stir until blended; set aside.

Brush some of melted butter over one sheet of phyllo; fold in half crosswise. (Cover remaining phyllo with a damp towel to prevent drying.) Press folded phyllo into a 9" pie plate, allowing ends to hang over edge of plate. Repeat with each sheet of phyllo and remaining butter, arranging phyllo at different angles in plate so bottom and sides are covered. Spoon turkey filling into phyllo crust. Fold ends of phyllo toward the center (crust will not cover center of filling). Bake uncovered for 45 to 50 minutes or until a knife inserted near the center comes out clean. Let stand 10 minutes before cutting into wedges.

* Use leftover roasted turkey, rotisserie chicken or frozen, fully cooked chicken breast strips.

Chicken Dinner in a Bag

serves 6

Ingredients

2 T. flour
1 large oven cooking bag (16 x 17½")
1 (1.3 oz.) env. dry golden onion soup mix
3 medium carrots, peeled

1 green bell pepper, cored and seeded
2 medium red potatoes
6 chicken pieces, skin removed
Seasoned salt and pepper to taste

Preparation

Preheat oven to 350°. Pour flour into oven bag and shake well. Place bag in a 9 x 13" baking pan (2" deep). Add soup mix and 1 cup water to bag and squeeze bag to blend in flour. Cut carrots and bell pepper into even chunks. Cut potatoes into wedges. Add carrots, bell pepper and potatoes to oven bag. Turn bag to coat ingredients with sauce. Sprinkle chicken with seasoned salt and pepper. Arrange chicken and vegetables in an even layer inside bag. Close bag with nylon tie. With a sharp knife or scissors, cut six ½" slits in top of bag to let steam escape. Tuck ends of bag into pan. Place pan in oven and bake for 55 to 60 minutes, until chicken is tender and juices run clear. Let stand 5 minutes.

With scissors, cut open the top of bag. Stir juices and serve with chicken and vegetables.

Chicken-Potato Bake

serves 4

Ingredients

1 (3 lb.) whole chicken,
  cut into pieces
1 lb. potatoes (2 large)
8 oz. baby carrots
½ C. Italian salad dressing

1 T. dried Italian seasoning
½ C. grated Parmesan cheese
Salt and pepper to taste

Preparation

Preheat oven to 400°. Grease a 9 x 13" baking dish with nonstick cooking spray. Place chicken pieces in prepared dish. Cut potatoes into small chunks and arrange around chicken. Scatter carrots around chicken. Drizzle dressing over all ingredients in dish; sprinkle with Italian seasoning and Parmesan cheese. Season with salt and pepper as desired. Cover dish with aluminum foil and bake for 40 minutes. Uncover and bake about 20 minutes longer or until vegetables are tender and chicken is cooked through.

Chicken may be marinated in Italian dressing for several hours in the refrigerator before assembly.

Southwest Roll-Ups

serves 10

Ingredients

1 to 2 jalapeño peppers, seeded
1 (15 oz.) can black beans, drained
2 T. tomato salsa
½ tsp. minced garlic
2 T. chopped onion
½ tsp. ground cumin
1 T. chopped fresh cilantro

1½ C. chopped frozen, grilled fajita chicken strips, thawed
1 C. shredded Cheddar cheese, divided
10 (6") flour tortillas
Sour cream
Additional salsa

Preparation

Preheat oven to 350°. Grease a 9 x 13" baking dish with nonstick cooking spray; set aside.

Finely chop jalapeño peppers and place in a medium bowl. Mash black beans and add to bowl. Add 2 tablespoons salsa, garlic, onion, cumin, cilantro and chicken. Stir in ½ cup cheese. Spread a portion of mixture over each tortilla. Roll up tortillas and place seam side down in prepared baking dish. Cover dish tightly with aluminum foil and bake for 20 minutes or until heated through. Remove from oven and sprinkle rolls with remaining ½ cup cheese; return to oven for 5 minutes or until cheese melts. Serve warm with sour cream and additional salsa.

You may substitute one can refried beans for the black beans. If using larger tortillas, make fewer roll ups.

Chicken Supreme

serves 4

Ingredients

4 boneless, skinless chicken breast halves

6 bacon strips

1 (14 oz.) can chicken broth

¾ C. uncooked white rice

1 (2 oz.) pkg. thinly sliced dried beef

Pepper to taste

1 (14.5 oz.) can French-style green beans, drained

1 (8 oz.) pkg. cream cheese, warmed slightly

1 (10.75 oz.) can cream of chicken or cream of mushroom soup

1 (16 oz.) container sour cream

Preparation

Preheat oven to 325°. Grease a 9 x 13" baking dish with nonstick cooking spray; set aside. Cut chicken into 1" chunks and slice bacon into small pieces; set aside.

Pour broth into prepared baking dish. Sprinkle rice evenly into broth. Arrange slices of dried beef over broth/rice mixture in pan (it may float). Layer uncooked bacon pieces over dried beef. Place chicken chunks on top of bacon and season with pepper as desired. Arrange green beans over chicken.

In a medium bowl, whisk together cream cheese, soup and sour cream until smooth; spread mixture over all ingredients in baking dish. Cover tightly with aluminum foil and bake for 2 hours or until chicken is thoroughly cooked and rice is tender.

This dish freezes well after baking for a quick and easy meal another day.

Chicken Noodle Hot Dish

serves 6

Ingredients

1 C. frozen peas or mixed vegetables

2 C. cubed frozen, grilled chicken breast strips

2 C. French fried onions, divided

2 C. uncooked curly egg noodles

1½ C. shredded Cheddar cheese, divided

1 (10.75 oz.) can cream of chicken soup

1½ C. milk

Preparation

In a large bowl, combine vegetables, chicken pieces, 1 cup onions, uncooked noodles and ½ cup cheese, tossing until well mixed; set aside.

In a separate bowl, mix soup and milk until smooth. Pour soup mixture over chicken mixture and stir to coat. Transfer to an ungreased 2-quart baking dish; cover and let stand while preheating oven to 400°. Bake covered for 30 minutes or until noodles are tender. Remove from oven and stir gently. Top with remaining 1 cup cheese and 1 cup onions. Return to oven and bake uncovered 5 to 10 minutes longer, until onions are golden brown. Let stand 5 minutes before serving.

Variation *To make Turkey Noodle Hot Dish, use 1¼ cup light Parmesan Alfredo sauce (such as Cheesy Ragu) in place of soup and reduce milk to 1 cup. Use shredded cooked turkey in place of chicken strips. This hot dish may be baked at 350°, but increase first baking time to approximately 40 minutes.*

Corn & Drumstick Scallop

serves 4

Ingredients

1 (15 oz.) can cream-style corn
1 C. milk
1 egg, lightly beaten
1 T. flour
6 green onions
6 to 8 chicken drumsticks

Paprika
Seasoned salt to taste
30 saltine crackers
¼ C. butter
1 (4 oz.) can sliced
   mushrooms, drained

Preparation

Preheat oven to 350°. Lightly grease a 9 x 13" baking dish with nonstick cooking spray. Pour corn, milk, egg and flour into prepared dish and stir well to combine. Slice green onions and tops; stir into corn mixture to distribute evenly. Sprinkle drumsticks generously with paprika and arrange chicken over corn mixture. Sprinkle with seasoned salt as desired.

Crush crackers and sprinkle on top. Dot evenly with pieces of butter. Bake uncovered for 1 hour or until chicken is tender. Remove from oven and arrange mushrooms in the center of casserole. Return to oven for 5 minutes or until heated through.

Homestyle Chicken & Biscuits

serves 6

Ingredients

2 C. diced cooked chicken
1 (16 oz.) pkg. frozen California blend vegetables (broccoli, cauliflower, carrots), thawed
1 (1.8 oz.) env. dry vegetable soup mix
½ tsp. dried Italian seasoning

¼ tsp. garlic powder
2 T. butter, divided
½ C. boiling chicken broth
1½ C. milk
1 (7.5 oz.) tube refrigerated buttermilk biscuits (not grand size)

Preparation

Preheat oven to 375°. Grease a 9" deep-dish pie plate or 9" square baking dish with nonstick cooking spray; set aside.

Place diced chicken in a large bowl. Add thawed vegetables, soup mix, Italian seasoning, garlic powder and 1 tablespoon butter; pour boiling broth over all and mix well. Stir in milk until blended. Pour mixture into prepared pie plate and bake uncovered for 25 minutes or until vegetables are tender.

Remove dish from oven and stir gently. Arrange biscuits over chicken mixture and dot with pieces of remaining 1 tablespoon butter. Return to oven and bake 12 to 15 minutes longer or until chicken mixture is bubbly and biscuits are golden brown. Let stand at least 5 minutes before serving.

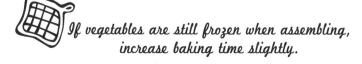
If vegetables are still frozen when assembling, increase baking time slightly.

Quick & Light Chicken Broccoli Casserole

serves 5

Ingredients

½ to ¾ (16 oz.) pkg. frozen broccoli florets, thawed

2 boneless, skinless chicken breast halves

½ C. lite mayonnaise

½ C. lite sour cream

4 tsp. dried minced onion, rehydrated in water

1 C. shredded Cheddar cheese

1 (8 oz.) can sliced water chestnuts, drained

1 C. crushed butter crackers

¼ C. melted butter, or less to taste

Preparation

Preheat oven to 350°. In an ungreased 8" square baking dish, spread thawed broccoli in a single layer to cover bottom of dish. Cut uncooked chicken into 1" strips and arrange over broccoli; set aside.

In a small bowl, stir together mayonnaise, sour cream and drained, rehydrated onion. Spread over chicken and broccoli. Sprinkle cheese over creamy layer and arrange water chestnuts on top. In a small bowl, mix cracker crumbs and melted butter; sprinkle over casserole. Bake uncovered for 30 to 35 minutes or until crumbs are golden brown and chicken is cooked through.

 This recipe doubles easily to fit a 9 x 13" baking dish.

Curried Chicken & Rice Packs

serves 4

Ingredients

4 boneless, skinless chicken breast halves

3 tsp. curry powder, divided

2 C. uncooked instant brown or white rice

2 C. frozen peas and carrots

2 C. chicken broth, divided

½ C. raisins, optional

Salt and pepper to taste

Preparation

Preheat oven to 450°. Cut four (12 x 18") pieces of heavy-duty aluminum foil; grease dull side of each piece with nonstick cooking spray. Place a chicken breast in the center of greased side of each foil piece. Sprinkle about ¼ teaspoon curry powder over each piece of chicken and set aside.

In a medium bowl, combine uncooked rice, peas and carrots, 1 cup chicken broth, remaining 2 teaspoons curry powder and raisins, if desired; mix well. Spoon a portion of rice mixture around each chicken breast.

To create a foil pack, bring up two opposite sides of foil and fold over twice to seal; seal one end in the same way. Through remaining open end, pour ¼ cup of remaining broth. Double-fold open end to seal packet well, leaving room for heat to circulate inside. Repeat the process to make three more sealed packs. Place packs on a cookie sheet and bake for 20 to 25 minutes or until chicken is cooked through. Let stand 5 minutes before cutting slits in foil to release steam. Season with salt and pepper as desired.

Chicken Cordon Bleu

serves 10

Ingredients

- 10 boneless, skinless chicken breast halves
- 10 slices Swiss cheese
- 10 thin slices deli ham
- 2 (10.75 oz.) cans cream of chicken soup
- ½ C. sour cream
- 2 C. herbed stuffing mix
- ⅓ C. melted butter

Preparation

Preheat oven to 350°. Grease a 9 x 13" baking dish with nonstick cooking spray; set aside.

Flatten chicken pieces to ¼" thickness.* Layer a slice of cheese and ham on each piece of chicken and roll up like a jelly roll. Fasten with wooden toothpicks as needed. Arrange chicken rolls in prepared baking dish and set aside.

In a medium bowl, whisk together both cans of soup, sour cream and 2 tablespoons water. Spread mixture over chicken rolls. Crush dry stuffing mix and place in a small bowl. Drizzle with melted butter and toss well. Sprinkle stuffing mixture over chicken. Bake uncovered for 1 hour or until chicken is fully cooked.

To flatten chicken breasts, pound with a meat mallet or place pieces in a heavy-duty resealable plastic bag and pound with the side of a heavy can until ¼" thick.

Easy Overnight Casserole

serves 8

Ingredients

3 (6 oz.) pkgs. frozen, grilled chicken breast strips

2 C. uncooked elbow macaroni

2 C. milk

2 (10.75 oz.) cans cream of mushroom or cream of chicken soup

½ C. Velveeta cheese, cubed

Pepper to taste, optional

Preparation

Grease a 9 x 13" baking dish with nonstick cooking spray; set aside.

Dice chicken strips to measure 3 to 4 cups. In a large bowl, stir together chicken, uncooked macaroni, milk, both cans of soup and cheese. Season with pepper, if desired. Cover dish tightly with aluminum foil and refrigerate overnight.

When ready to bake, preheat oven to 350°. Bake covered for 1½ hours or until pasta is tender and casserole is bubbly. Uncover the last 10 minutes of baking time.

Variation
Try frozen Italian-style or fajita grilled chicken breast strips for a different flavor, or use rotisserie or leftover cooked chicken or turkey in place of frozen chicken strips.

Foil Pack Fajitas

serves 4

Ingredients

1½ C. uncooked instant
   white rice

1½ C. hot water

1 T. taco seasoning mix

4 boneless, skinless chicken
   breast halves

1 green bell pepper,
   cored and seeded

1 red bell pepper,
   cored and seeded

½ C. chunky tomato salsa

½ C. shredded taco
   blend cheese

Sour cream, optional

Preparation

Preheat oven to 400°. Cut four (12 x 18") pieces of heavy-duty
aluminum foil; fold up edges to form a 1" rim. Grease foil with
nonstick cooking spray. In a medium bowl, mix uncooked rice, hot
water and seasoning mix. Spoon a portion of rice mixture onto each
piece of foil and top with a chicken breast; set aside.

Slice both bell peppers into thin strips and arrange strips over
chicken. Top each serving with a portion of salsa and cheese. To
create a foil pack, bring up two opposite sides of foil and fold over
twice to seal; seal both open ends in the same way. Place packs
on a cookie sheet and bake for 30 to 35 minutes or until chicken is
cooked through. Let stand 5 minutes before cutting slits in foil to
release steam. Serve with sour cream, if desired.

Bruschetta-Stuffed Chicken

serves 8

Ingredients

1 (14.5 oz.) can fire-roasted diced tomatoes with garlic, with juice

1¼ C. shredded mozzarella cheese, divided

¼ C. chopped fresh basil

2½ C. stuffing mix for chicken (or scant 6 oz. pkg.)

8 boneless, skinless chicken breast halves

⅓ C. Italian salad dressing

Grated Parmesan cheese

Preparation

In a medium bowl, combine tomatoes, ½ cup mozzarella cheese and basil. Add dry stuffing mix and stir until moistened. With a sharp knife, slice each chicken breast from thickest side toward, but not through, opposite edge so pieces open like a book. Fill opening with a mound of stuffing mixture, pressing in place with hands as needed. Partially close chicken around stuffing and secure with wooden toothpicks as needed. Place in a 9 x 13" baking dish, stuffing side up. Drizzle with dressing and sprinkle lightly with Parmesan cheese. Bake immediately, or cover and refrigerate several hours.

When ready to bake, preheat oven to 350°. Bake for 35 to 40 minutes or until chicken juices run clear and stuffing is browned. Sprinkle with remaining ¾ cup mozzarella cheese and return to oven for 5 minutes longer to melt cheese.

Any extra stuffing may be added to the bottom of baking dish around chicken or heated separately in the microwave to serve on the side.

Fiesta Chicken

serves 4

Ingredients

2 T. flour

1 large oven cooking bag (16 x 17½")

1 (14.5 oz.) can diced tomatoes with juice

2 to 3 tsp. finely chopped jalapeño pepper

1 tsp. chili powder

½ tsp. ground oregano

¼ tsp. cayenne pepper

½ tsp. salt

1 (15 oz.) can black beans, rinsed and drained

6 chicken pieces, skin removed

1 yellow bell pepper, cored and seeded

½ green bell pepper, cored and seeded

Preparation

Preheat oven to 350°. Pour flour into oven bag and shake well. Place bag in a 9 x 13" baking pan (2" deep). Add tomatoes, jalapeño pepper, chili powder, oregano, cayenne pepper and salt; squeeze bag gently to blend. Add black beans and chicken to bag and turn bag to coat chicken with sauce. Arrange ingredients in an even layer in bag. Slice yellow and green bell peppers and place on top of food in bag. Close bag with nylon tie. With a sharp knife or scissors, cut six ½" slits in top of bag to let steam escape. Tuck ends of bag into pan. Place pan in oven and bake for 45 to 50 minutes or until chicken is tender. Let stand 10 minutes.

With scissors, cut open the top of bag and carefully remove food.

Seafood

Baked Fish & Rice

serves 4

Ingredients

½ C. uncooked white rice
¼ tsp. dried Italian seasoning
¼ tsp. garlic powder
1½ C. boiling chicken broth
1 (10 oz.) pkg. frozen chopped broccoli, thawed and drained
1 T. grated Parmesan cheese
1 (2.8 oz.) can French-fried onions, divided

1 lb. fresh or frozen fish fillets, thawed
Paprika to taste
Onion powder to taste
Seasoned salt to taste
Dried dill weed, optional
½ C. shredded Cheddar cheese

Preparation

Preheat oven to 375°. Grease a 7 x 11" baking dish with nonstick cooking spray. In prepared dish, combine uncooked rice, Italian seasoning, garlic powder and boiling broth; stir to blend. Cover dish tightly with aluminum foil and bake for 10 minutes.

Remove dish from oven and add broccoli. Sprinkle with Parmesan cheese and half the onions. Top with fish fillets; sprinkle with paprika, onion powder, seasoned salt and dill weed as desired. Cover and return to oven to bake 20 to 25 minutes longer or until fish flakes easily with a fork. Uncover and sprinkle with Cheddar cheese and remaining onions. Return to oven for 5 minutes or until cheese is melted.

Seafood

Salmon Hot Dish

serves 8

Ingredients

1 (14.7 oz.) can salmon
1 (14.7 oz.) can cream-style corn
½ C. evaporated milk
2 eggs, slightly beaten
¼ tsp. salt
Dash of pepper

1 T. melted butter
⅓ C. fine dry bread crumbs
½ C. shredded Cheddar cheese
1 T. finely chopped fresh chives
   or parsley

Preparation

Preheat oven to 375°. Lightly grease an 8" square baking dish with nonstick cooking spray and set aside. Drain salmon, reserving liquid. Place salmon in a medium bowl; flake with a fork, discarding bones and skin. Add reserved liquid, corn, evaporated milk, eggs, salt and pepper to bowl; blend well. Pour mixture into prepared baking dish and set aside.

In a small bowl, combine melted butter, bread crumbs, cheese and chives; sprinkle over salmon mixture in dish. Bake for 25 to 30 minutes or until golden brown.

Seafood Lasagna

serves 6

Ingredients

1 (15 oz.) container ricotta cheese

1 (8 oz.) pkg. cream cheese, softened

1 C. finely chopped onion

2 tsp. dried basil

½ tsp. salt

⅛ tsp. pepper

1 egg

1 (10.75 oz.) can cream of mushroom soup

1 (10.75 oz.) can cream of shrimp soup

⅓ C. milk

½ C. chicken broth or white wine

1 tsp. minced garlic

½ lb. scallops, patted dry

½ lb. cubed flounder or tilapia

2 (4 oz.) cans tiny shrimp, drained

16 no-boil lasagna noodles (9 to 10 oz.), divided

1 C. shredded mozzarella cheese

¼ C. grated Parmesan cheese

Preparation

Preheat oven to 350°. Grease a 9 x 13" baking dish with nonstick cooking spray; set aside.

In a medium bowl, mix ricotta cheese, cream cheese, onion, basil, salt, pepper and egg; set aside. In a large bowl, stir together both cans of soup, milk, broth and garlic. Add scallops, flounder and shrimp; toss until evenly coated and set aside.

Spread a thin layer of seafood mixture over bottom of prepared dish. In layers, top seafood mixture with four uncooked lasagna noodles, half the ricotta mixture, four noodles, half the remaining seafood mixture, four noodles, remaining ricotta mixture, and remaining noodles and seafood mixture. Cover dish with aluminum foil that has been sprayed with nonstick cooking spray and bake for 30 minutes.

Remove from oven and top with mozzarella and Parmesan cheeses. Bake uncovered for 20 to 30 minutes longer or until fully cooked. Let stand 10 minutes before serving.

Seafood

Crab-Stuffed Zucchini

serves 6

Ingredients

3 medium zucchini
1 (6 oz.) can crabmeat, drained
½ C. finely chopped onion
½ tsp. garlic powder
½ C. shredded Swiss cheese
⅓ C. crumbled feta cheese

1 egg, lightly beaten
1 T. flour
¾ tsp. dried parsley
½ tsp. dried dill weed
1 tsp. paprika
¼ tsp. pepper

Preparation

Preheat oven to 375°. Grease a jelly roll pan with nonstick cooking spray; set aside.

Cut zucchini in half lengthwise and scoop out pulp, leaving ½"-thick shells. Arrange shells in a single layer on prepared jelly roll pan. Chop zucchini pulp and place in a medium bowl. Remove cartilage from crabmeat; flake the meat with a fork and add to bowl with zucchini. Add onion, garlic powder, Swiss cheese, feta cheese, egg, flour, parsley, dill weed, paprika and pepper; stir well. Spoon a portion of crab mixture into each zucchini shell. Bake uncovered about 30 minutes or until filling is set.

Tropical Rice & Salmon

serves 4

Ingredients

1 C. uncooked instant white or brown rice

1 C. boiling chicken broth

1 T. cracked coriander seed* or 1½ tsp. ground coriander

1 T. brown sugar

1 tsp. lemon pepper seasoning

1 (15 oz.) can tropical fruit salad, drained

1 tsp. dried cilantro

½ to 1 tsp. finely grated lemon zest

4 (3 to 4 oz.) frozen salmon fillets, thawed

1 T. melted butter

Preparation

Lightly grease an 8" square baking dish with nonstick cooking spray. Place uncooked rice in prepared dish and stir in boiling broth. Cover dish tightly with aluminum foil and place in cold oven. Set oven temperature to 425° and allow rice to cook for 15 minutes as oven preheats.

Meanwhile, in a small bowl, mix coriander seed, brown sugar and lemon-pepper seasoning; set aside. Dice tropical fruit and set aside.

Remove rice from oven and add fruit, cilantro and lemon zest; stir until well combined. Arrange salmon fillets over rice mixture and brush tops with melted butter. Sprinkle coriander mixture evenly over fish, pressing it gently in place. Cover dish with foil and return to oven to bake for 15 to 20 minutes. Remove from oven and let stand 5 minutes. Fish should flake easily with a fork and rice should be tender.

* Crack whole coriander seeds in a garlic press or place seeds in a resealable plastic bag and pound lightly. For added flavor, toast the seeds first.

Seafood

Baked Seafood Casserole

serves 4

Ingredients

6 to 8 oz. crabmeat, drained
1 (4 oz.) can tiny shrimp, drained
6 C. cubed French or
  Italian bread
¼ C. chopped fresh parsley
1 C. diced Cheddar cheese

4 eggs
2 C. milk
1 C. half & half
¼ C. melted butter
2 tsp. dry mustard
½ C. shredded Cheddar cheese

Preparation

Grease a 2½-quart baking dish with nonstick cooking spray; set aside. Remove cartilage from crabmeat. Flake the meat with a fork and place in a small bowl. Stir in shrimp and set aside. In a large bowl, combine bread cubes, parsley and diced cheese; toss to blend. In prepared baking dish, alternately layer seafood and bread mixtures, using about ¼ of each mixture for each layer.

In a medium bowl, lightly beat eggs. Whisk in milk, half & half, melted butter, dry mustard and shredded cheese. Pour milk mixture over ingredients in dish. Cover and chill for 1 hour.

When ready to bake, preheat oven to 350°. Bake casserole for 1 hour or until puffed and golden.

Tuna Crunch

serves 6

Ingredients

1 (4 oz.) can shoestring
  potatoes, divided

1 (6.4 oz.) pouch tuna*

1 (10.75 oz.) can cream of
  mushroom soup

1 (5 oz.) can evaporated milk

1½ C. frozen peas,
  slightly thawed

¼ C. diced pimiento

1 (4 oz.) can sliced mushrooms,
  drained, optional

Preparation

Preheat oven to 375°. Lightly grease a 1½-quart casserole dish with nonstick cooking spray; set aside.

Reserve 1 cup shoestring potatoes for casserole topping. Place remaining potatoes in a large bowl. Add tuna, soup and evaporated milk; stir well to blend. Fold in peas, pimiento and mushrooms, if desired. Pour mixture into prepared casserole dish. Top with reserved potatoes. Bake for 25 minutes or until hot.

* If using canned tuna, drain well before combining with other
  ingredients.

Seafood Sandwich

serves 8

Ingredients

1 loaf Italian or country-style bread

½ C. butter, softened

1 tsp. dried dill weed

¼ tsp. salt, plus more for seasoning fish

¼ tsp. onion powder

Dash of pepper

½ tsp. minced garlic

12 oz. fresh or frozen salmon, thawed

8 oz. fresh or frozen haddock or tilapia, thawed

8 oz. fresh mushrooms

8 oz. crabmeat, drained, cartilage removed

3 to 4 T. white wine, chicken broth or apple juice

Preparation

Preheat oven to 350°. Line a cookie sheet with aluminum foil. Hollow out the loaf of bread and place bread shell on prepared sheet. By hand or with a food processor, crumble the bread removed from inside of loaf to make fresh bread crumbs; reserve for topping.

In a small bowl, mix butter, dill weed, ¼ teaspoon salt, onion powder, pepper and garlic. Reserve 2 tablespoons of butter mixture; spread remaining mixture inside hollowed-out loaf and set aside. Cut salmon and haddock into bite-size pieces; place fish in a bowl and toss well with a little salt. Slice mushrooms into bowl with fish. Add crabmeat and mix well. Stuff fish mixture into prepared bread shell. Pack most of reserved bread crumbs on top of fish. Place dollops of reserved butter mixture over bread crumbs. Drizzle entire loaf with wine. Bake approximately 1 hour or until fish is cooked through and loaf is very crusty. Slice to serve.

Seafood

Scalloped Shrimp & Corn

serves 8

Ingredients

2 eggs
1¼ C. milk
1 tsp. dried minced onion
¼ tsp. Beau Monde seasoning
1 tsp. dried tarragon
1 (15 oz.) can cream-style corn
¼ C. finely chopped celery

¼ C. finely chopped
   green bell pepper
1 (4 oz.) can tiny shrimp, drained
22 saltine crackers
1 T. melted butter
Green bell pepper rings, optional

Preparation

Preheat oven to 350°. In a 2-quart casserole dish, whisk together eggs and milk. Add onion, Beau Monde seasoning, tarragon, corn, celery, bell pepper and shrimp; stir until combined and set aside.

Finely crush crackers and place in a small bowl. Remove approximately ⅔ of cracker crumbs and stir into corn mixture. Drizzle melted butter over remaining crumbs in bowl and toss to coat. Sprinkle crumbs over corn mixture. Bake uncovered for 1 hour or until a knife inserted in the center comes out clean. Top with bell pepper rings before serving, if desired.

Orange Roughy with Rice Pilaf

Ingredients

1 C. uncooked white rice
1 T. butter
2 C. boiling chicken broth
¼ C. sliced green onions
¼ C. finely chopped celery
¼ C. chopped carrots
4 fresh or frozen orange roughy or tilapia fillets, thawed
Salt and pepper to taste

Garlic powder to taste
2 C. fresh baby spinach leaves
1 C. sliced fresh mushrooms
1 C. chopped tomato
1 C. sliced artichoke hearts, optional
⅓ C. Italian or sun-dried tomato vinaigrette salad dressing

Preparation

Preheat oven to 375°. Place rice and butter in a greased 1-quart casserole dish. Pour boiling broth over rice and stir until butter melts. Stir in green onions, celery and carrots. Cover dish tightly with aluminum foil and place on upper rack in oven to begin baking.

Meanwhile, grease a 9 x 13" baking dish with nonstick cooking spray; arrange orange roughy fillets in prepared dish. Season with salt, pepper and garlic powder. In a large bowl, combine spinach, mushrooms, tomato, artichokes, if desired, and dressing; spoon mixture over fish. Place dish on lower rack in oven with partially baked rice pilaf. Bake uncovered for 20 to 25 minutes or until fish flakes easily with a fork and rice is tender. Fluff rice with a fork before serving alongside fish and vegetables.

Variation
Try this recipe with salmon, chicken breasts, asparagus spears, and/or roasted red pepper/Parmesan salad dressing.

Chinese Tuna Casserole

serves 6

Ingredients

1 (6.4 oz.) pouch tuna*
2 C. chow mein noodles
1 C. chopped celery
½ C. chopped onion
¼ C. chopped green bell pepper

½ C. chopped cashews
1 (10.75 oz.) can cream of
  mushroom soup
⅔ C. crushed potato chips

Preparation

Preheat oven to 350°. Lightly grease a 1½-quart casserole dish with nonstick cooking spray; set aside.

In a large bowl, combine tuna, noodles, celery, onion, bell pepper and cashews. In a separate bowl, mix soup and ⅔ cup water until blended. Pour soup mixture over tuna mixture and stir lightly to coat. Pour into prepared casserole dish and sprinkle potato chips on top. Bake uncovered for 35 to 40 minutes or until hot and bubbly.

* If using canned tuna, drain well before combining with other
  ingredients.

Parchment Pack Salmon

serves 4

Ingredients

½ C. mayonnaise
¼ C. Dijon mustard
¼ C. chopped fresh dill weed
¼ C. chopped fresh tarragon
2 tsp. lemon juice
2 tsp. finely grated lemon zest
2 tsp. minced garlic

1 tsp. soy sauce
Hot pepper sauce to taste
Salt and white pepper to taste
4 fresh or frozen salmon
   fillets, thawed
16 asparagus spears
Vegetable oil

Preparation

Preheat oven to 400°. In a small bowl, mix mayonnaise, Dijon mustard, dill weed, tarragon, lemon juice, lemon zest, garlic and soy sauce. Season with pepper sauce, salt and pepper. Spread mayonnaise mixture on all sides of fillets and set aside.

Cut four 15" squares of parchment paper; brush one side with vegetable oil. Place four asparagus spears on half of each paper; set salmon on asparagus. Fold paper over food, like closing a book. To seal packs, narrowly fold cut edges three times; crease well. Fold corners under. Place packs on a cookie sheet and bake for 10 to 15 minutes or until salmon is fully cooked and asparagus is crisp-tender. Cut an "X" in the top of each pack and tear open to serve.

Variation
Omit mayonnaise mixture. Brush fillets with olive oil and sprinkle with lemon pepper and dill weed; top with a slice of lemon, lime and orange. Place each fillet in a parchment pouch, adding ⅔ cup frozen green beans next to fish before sealing. Bake at 425° for 12 to 15 minutes.

Tuna Pierogi Bake

serves 4

Ingredients

16 oz. frozen potato
   and cheese pierogies
4 tsp. dried, chopped onion
1 celery stalk
1 (5 oz.) can tuna, drained
1 (10.75 oz.) can cream of
   mushroom soup

1 T. mayonnaise
1 T. chopped pimiento, optional
1 C. crushed corn flakes cereal
4 slices American cheese

Preparation

Preheat oven to 350°. Grease an 8" square baking dish with nonstick cooking spray; set aside. Place pierogies in a large bowl and cover with very hot water; let stand for 5 minutes to thaw. In a small bowl, cover onion with water and let stand to rehydrate.

Finely chop celery and place in a medium bowl. Add tuna, soup, mayonnaise and pimiento, if desired; stir well. Drain pierogies and onion and add to tuna mixture; stir gently to coat. Spread pierogi mixture in prepared baking dish. Sprinkle with crushed cereal and arrange cheese slices on top. Bake uncovered approximately 35 minutes or until cheese begins to brown and casserole is hot and bubbly. Let stand several minutes before serving.

Variations *Swap out the American cheese for shredded Cheddar or Colby Jack cheese, or replace the cereal topping with French fried onion rings or soft bread crumbs tossed with melted butter. This recipe can be easily doubled for a 9x13" baking dish.*

 Low fat soup, mayonnaise and cheese may be used satisfactorily in this recipe.

Stuffed Trout with Green Beans

Ingredients

½ lb. fresh green beans*
Olive oil
Salt and pepper to taste
1 C. soft bread crumbs
½ C. minced sweet onion
2 T. chopped fresh dill weed

2 tsp. lemon zest
1 tsp. minced garlic
Salt and pepper to taste
4 fresh trout, cleaned,
   head removed
Lemon pepper seasoning

Preparation

Line a 9 x 13" baking pan with aluminum foil. Arrange green beans on foil, drizzle with olive oil and season with salt and pepper. Place pan in cold oven and set oven temperature to 400°. Roast green beans for approximately 10 minutes as oven preheats.

Meanwhile, in a medium bowl, toss bread crumbs with onion, dill weed, lemon zest, garlic and 2 tablespoons olive oil. Season with salt and pepper. Press a portion of stuffing into each trout. Brush fish with 2 tablespoons olive oil and sprinkle with lemon pepper seasoning. Remove green beans from oven and place fish on top. Bake uncovered for 15 to 20 minutes or until skin of fish begins to brown, flesh flakes easily with a fork and green beans are crisp-tender. Let stand 5 minutes before serving.

Frozen green beans will require 10 to 15 minutes more cooking time.

Variation *Toss thinly sliced red potatoes with olive oil, arrange on prepared pan and roast in oven during preheating. Prepare stuffing, adding ¼ cup toasted pine nuts; stuff fish as directed. Arrange asparagus spears over potatoes and top with stuffed fish; bake as directed.*

Haddock & Veggie Bake

serves 6

Ingredients

Fresh spinach leaves
½ C. olive oil, divided
6 fresh or frozen haddock or halibut fillets, thawed
Salt and pepper to taste
4 roma tomatoes
1 red bell pepper, cored and seeded

1 yellow bell pepper, cored and seeded
1 C. chopped red onion
5 T. capers or chopped artichoke hearts
6 T. chopped fresh basil or parsley
6 T. lemon juice

Preparation

Preheat oven to 400°. Line the bottom of a 7 x 11" baking dish with a bed of spinach leaves. Drizzle about 2 tablespoons olive oil over spinach. Arrange fish fillets on spinach and season with salt and pepper. Slice tomatoes and both bell peppers; place sliced vegetables on top of fish. Sprinkle evenly with red onion, capers and basil. Drizzle fish pieces with remaining 6 tablespoons olive oil and lemon juice. Cover dish tightly with aluminum foil and bake for 20 to 25 minutes or until fish flakes easily with a fork. Let stand 5 minutes before serving.

Variation *Assemble and wrap each serving of fish and vegetables in its own foil pack or place in individual baking dishes; bake as directed.*

Eggs

Oven Omelet

serves 6

Ingredients

5 whole eggs
10 egg whites
1 C. milk
¼ tsp. seasoned salt
¼ tsp. pepper
1½ C. fully cooked cubed ham

1 C. chopped fresh broccoli
1 C. shredded Cheddar cheese
1 fresh tomato, seeded
 and chopped
3 T. finely chopped onion

Preparation

Preheat oven to 350°. Grease a 10" ovenproof skillet with nonstick cooking spray; set aside.

In a medium bowl, combine whole eggs, egg whites, milk, seasoned salt and pepper; whisk until well blended. Pour mixture into prepared skillet. Sprinkle ham, broccoli, cheese, tomato and onion over eggs. Bake uncovered for 30 to 35 minutes or until eggs are almost set. Broil 4" to 6" from heat for 1 to 2 minutes or until eggs are set and top is lightly browned.

Next Day Savory Eggs

 serves 4

Ingredients

6 eggs
¼ tsp. salt
1 tsp. dry mustard

½ C. milk
½ cubed Velveeta cheese
Fresh chives to taste

Preparation

Grease an 8" square baking dish with nonstick cooking spray; set aside.

In a medium bowl, beat eggs. Whisk in salt, dry mustard and milk until blended. Stir in cheese and chives. Pour into prepared baking dish, cover and refrigerate overnight.

When ready to bake, preheat oven to 325°. Bake for 20 to 25 minutes, stirring after 10 minutes. Cooked eggs may be kept warm in a slow cooker for serving.

This recipe is easily doubled or tripled but will need a larger baking dish, longer baking time and more stirring.

Chile Rellenos Casserole

serves 4

Ingredients

1 C. finely chopped onion

2 (4 oz.) cans diced green chiles, drained

1½ C. shredded Cheddar cheese

1½ C. shredded Monterey Jack cheese

3 whole eggs

2 egg whites

¾ C. sour cream

¼ tsp. red pepper flakes, or to taste

1 C. chopped tomato

Preparation

Preheat oven to 350°. Lightly grease an 8" or 9" square baking dish. Spread onion and chiles over bottom of prepared dish. Sprinkle with Cheddar and Monterey Jack cheeses; set aside.

In a small bowl, lightly beat together whole eggs and egg whites. Add sour cream and red pepper flakes; beat until blended. Spoon egg mixture evenly over cheeses in pan. Sprinkle tomato pieces on top. Bake for 35 to 45 minutes or until a knife inserted near the center comes out clean. Let stand several minutes before slicing.

Eggs

Overnight Blueberry French Toast

serves 8

Ingredients

12 slices dry white bread
2 (8 oz.) pkgs. cream cheese
1 C. fresh or frozen blueberries
12 eggs

2 C. milk
½ C. maple syrup
Flavored syrups to serve
(blueberry, maple)

Preparation

Grease a 9 x 13" baking dish with nonstick cooking spray. Cut bread into ½" cubes (about 8 cups). Cut cream cheese into ¾" cubes. Arrange half the bread cubes over bottom of prepared dish. Sprinkle cream cheese pieces and blueberries evenly over bread. Arrange remaining bread cubes over blueberries; set aside.

In a large bowl, whisk eggs. Beat in milk and maple syrup. Carefully pour egg mixture over ingredients in dish. Cover with aluminum foil and refrigerate for at least 2 hours or up to 24 hours.

When ready to bake, preheat oven to 375°. Bake covered for 25 minutes. Uncover and bake about 25 minutes more or until a knife inserted near the center comes out clean and topping is puffed and golden brown. Let stand 10 minutes before serving. Serve warm with heated flavored syrups.

Eggs

Easy Brunch Bake

serves 12

Ingredients

12 slices white bread, divided
1 lb. kielbasa sausage
½ onion
1 red or green bell pepper, cored and seeded
8 oz. frozen corn, thawed and drained, divided

3 C. shredded Cheddar cheese, divided
½ C. thinly sliced green onions, divided
12 eggs
4 C. half & half
1 tsp. salt
¼ tsp. pepper

Preparation

Grease a 9 x 13" baking dish with nonstick cooking spray. Line the bottom of prepared dish with six slices of bread. Thinly slice the sausage; chop onion and bell pepper. Scatter half each of the sausage, onion, bell pepper and corn over bread. Top with half the cheese and half the green onions.

In a large bowl, whisk eggs with half & half, salt and pepper until blended. Pour 1 cup egg mixture over ingredients in dish. Cube remaining bread and arrange over eggs. Repeat layers with remaining sausage, onion, bell pepper, corn, cheese and green onions. Slowly pour remaining egg mixture evenly over top. Cover with plastic wrap. Place three 15-ounce cans on top of casserole for at least 15 minutes to submerge ingredients.

When ready to bake, preheat oven to 325°. Uncover and bake for 50 to 60 minutes or until set. If desired, broil until top is puffy and golden brown, about 5 minutes. Let stand 10 minutes before serving.

After assembling, casserole may be refrigerated overnight. Bring to room temperature before baking.

Broccoli-Bacon Strata

serves 6

Ingredients

4 C. cubed English muffins
(about 4 muffins), divided

1 (3 oz.) pkg. real bacon bits
(about ¾ C.)

1 C. fully cooked diced ham

1 (10 oz.) pkg. frozen chopped
broccoli, thawed and drained*

1 C. shredded Swiss or Gruyère
cheese, shredded

4 eggs

¼ C. sour cream

1¼ C. milk

2 T. finely chopped onion

1 T. Dijon mustard

⅛ tsp. pepper

Preparation

Grease an 8" square baking dish with nonstick cooking spray. Arrange 2 cups English muffin pieces over bottom of prepared dish. Top with layers of bacon, ham, broccoli and cheese. Arrange remaining 2 cups muffin pieces over the top and set aside.

In a medium bowl, beat eggs. Whisk in sour cream until blended. Stir in milk, onion, Dijon mustard and pepper. Pour mixture evenly over ingredients in dish. Cover dish tightly and refrigerate for up to 24 hours.

When ready to bake, preheat oven to 325°. Bake uncovered for 60 to 65 minutes or until set and cooked through. Let stand 10 minutes before serving.

You may use fresh broccoli or asparagus pieces in place of frozen.

Sausage-Egg Bake

serves 10

Ingredients

1 lb. ground breakfast sausage
8 eggs, lightly beaten
2 (12 oz.) cans evaporated milk
2 C. shredded Cheddar cheese
½ C. chopped red bell pepper
¼ C. thinly sliced green onions

½ tsp. onion powder
¼ tsp. garlic powder
Salt and pepper to taste
8 C. cubed Italian or French bread (about 9 slices)

Preparation

Preheat oven to 350°. Lightly grease a 9 x 13" baking dish with nonstick cooking spray. Crumble uncooked sausage evenly over bottom of prepared dish; set aside.

In a large bowl, whisk together eggs and evaporated milk. Add cheese, bell pepper, green onions, onion powder, garlic powder, salt and pepper; stir until well blended. Add bread cubes and stir until moistened. Pour egg mixture over sausage in dish. Bake for 50 to 55 minutes or until set and sausage is fully cooked.

South-of-the-Border Breakfast

serves 10

Ingredients

5 C. frozen shredded hash brown potatoes, thawed
3 C. fully cooked diced ham
1 C. chopped green bell pepper
3 C. shredded Mexican blend cheese, divided
5 eggs

1¼ C. sour cream, divided
1 C. milk
1 tsp. dried oregano
1 tsp. salt
½ tsp. chili powder, or to taste
½ tsp. onion powder
¾ C. pico de gallo

Preparation

Preheat oven to 350°. Grease a 9 x 13" baking dish with nonstick cooking spray; set aside.

In a large bowl, combine potatoes, ham, bell pepper and 2 cups cheese; set aside. In a medium bowl, whisk together eggs, 1 cup sour cream, milk, oregano, salt, chili powder and onion powder. Pour egg mixture into potato mixture and stir to blend; spread in prepared baking dish. Bake uncovered for 35 minutes.

Remove dish from oven and sprinkle with remaining 1 cup cheese. Return to oven and bake for 15 to 20 minutes more or until potatoes are tender and knife inserted in the center comes out clean. Let stand several minutes before slicing; top pieces with a spoonful of pico de gallo and a small dollop of remaining ¼ cup sour cream.

Canadian Bacon Quiche

serves 8

Ingredients

3 to 4 slices Swiss cheese
1 ready-to-bake pie shell
½ C. chopped fresh spinach
½ C. sliced canned
    mushrooms, drained
3 eggs

1 C. half & half
2 T. flour
½ tsp. salt
4 oz. Canadian bacon
½ C. shredded Swiss
    or Cheddar cheese

Preparation

Preheat oven to 350°. Place cheese slices in bottom of pie shell. Arrange spinach over cheese. Cover with mushrooms and set aside.

In a medium bowl, beat together eggs, half & half, flour and salt until blended. Pour egg mixture over mushrooms. Chop Canadian bacon and sprinkle meat over eggs. Top with shredded cheese. Bake for 45 to 55 minutes or until set and golden brown.

Broccoli Brunch Pie

Ingredients

4 C. Corn Chex cereal
5 T. melted butter
1 tsp. ground oregano
1 (10 oz.) pkg. frozen chopped
  broccoli, thawed and drained
2 T. flour

½ C. chopped onion
3 eggs, beaten
1 C. half & half
½ tsp. salt
1 C. shredded Cheddar cheese

Preparation

Preheat oven to 350°. Grease a 9" pie plate with nonstick cooking spray; set aside. Crush cereal to measure 1 cup and place in a small bowl. Add melted butter and oregano; stir until evenly coated. Press mixture into bottom and up sides of prepared pie plate. Bake for 8 to 10 minutes; remove from oven.

Meanwhile, in a medium bowl, mix broccoli, flour, onion, eggs, half & half and salt. Slowly pour mixture into partially baked pie shell. Sprinkle cheese over top. Bake for 40 to 50 minutes or until a knife inserted near the center comes out clean.

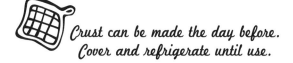

Crust can be made the day before. Cover and refrigerate until use.

Eggs Benedict Breakfast Pizza

Ingredients

12 eggs, well beaten
1¼ C. milk
½ tsp. salt
2 (8 oz.) tubes refrigerated crescent rolls

1 (7.5 oz.) jar hollandaise sauce
3 C. fully cooked diced ham
1 C. chopped onion
1½ C. shredded Cheddar cheese

Preparation

Preheat oven to 350°. Grease an 8" square baking dish with nonstick cooking spray; set aside.

In a large bowl, whisk together eggs, milk and salt until blended. Pour egg mixture into prepared baking dish and bake uncovered for 25 to 35 minutes or until eggs are set, stirring several times during cooking.

When eggs are done, remove dish from oven and set aside. Increase oven temperature to 375°. Unroll crescent rolls and place on an ungreased 12" pizza pan or baking stone, with points toward the center. Press seams together and press edges of dough to form a rim on crust. Pre-bake crust for 5 minutes.

Remove partially baked crust from oven and spread desired amount of hollandaise sauce evenly over crust. Arrange scrambled eggs over sauce. Top with ham, onion and cheese. Return to oven and bake 15 to 20 minutes longer or until crust is lightly browned.

Meatless

Fajita Lasagna

serves 8

Ingredients

1 (16 oz.) pkg. frozen stir-fry bell peppers and onions, thawed

1 (12 oz.) pkg. frozen ground beef substitute,* thawed

1 (29 oz.) can tomato sauce

1 (1.4 oz.) env. fajita seasoning mix

12 no-boil lasagna noodles (7 to 8 oz.), divided

3 C. shredded Colby Jack cheese, divided

1 (2¼ oz.) can sliced black olives, drained

Guacamole, optional

Tomato salsa, optional

Sour cream, optional

Preparation

Preheat oven to 350°. Grease a 9 x 13" baking dish with nonstick cooking spray. Drain thawed vegetables on paper towels; set aside.

In a medium bowl, stir together uncooked ground beef substitute, tomato sauce and seasoning mix. Spread ½ cup sauce mixture in prepared baking dish. Arrange four noodles crosswise on sauce, overlapping slightly; cover with 1½ cups sauce mixture. Spread vegetables evenly over sauce; sprinkle with 1 cup cheese. Make another layer of four noodles, 1½ cups sauce mixture and 1 cup cheese. Sprinkle with olives. Arrange remaining four noodles over olives and cover with remaining sauce mixture and 1 cup cheese.

Cover dish with aluminum foil that has been sprayed with nonstick cooking spray. Bake about 30 minutes or until hot and bubbly. Let stand 15 minutes before cutting. Serve with guacamole, salsa and sour cream as desired.

* Such as beef-flavored crumbles from Morning Star, Gimme Lean or other brands.

Cheesy Zucchini Casserole

serves 6

Ingredients

1 medium yellow squash
2 small to medium zucchini
1 egg, lightly beaten
1½ C. milk
½ C. chopped onion
1 C. uncooked instant white rice

½ C. shredded Cheddar cheese
1 tsp. Italian seasoning
½ tsp. salt
½ tsp. pepper
Dash of garlic salt
½ to ¾ c. shredded Swiss cheese

Preparation

Preheat oven to 375°. Grease a 2-quart casserole dish or 8" baking dish with nonstick cooking spray; set aside.

Slice squash and zucchini crosswise into ¼"-thick rounds; set aside. In a medium bowl, mix egg and milk. Add onion, uncooked rice, Cheddar cheese, Italian seasoning, salt, pepper and garlic salt; stir until blended. Pour rice mixture into prepared casserole dish. Place squash and zucchini slices on edge in rice mixture, alternating colors and overlapping slices until rice is covered. Sprinkle Swiss cheese over top. Bake uncovered for 35 minutes or until lightly browned and all liquid is absorbed. Let stand several minutes before serving.

Meatless

Spicy Mac & Cheese

serves 6

Ingredients

2 C. uncooked elbow macaroni
½ C. milk
1 (14.5 oz.) can chicken broth
1½ C. shredded Cheddar or
   Colby Jack cheese
½ C. shredded Pepper Jack
   cheese

4 oz. spreadable chive
   and onion cream cheese
1 tsp. onion salt
½ tsp. dry mustard
2 T. flour
Pepper to taste

Preparation

Preheat oven to 350°. Grease a deep 1½-quart casserole dish with nonstick cooking spray; set aside.

In a large bowl, stir together uncooked macaroni, milk and broth until well blended. Add both shredded cheeses, cream cheese, onion salt, dry mustard and flour; mix well. Season with pepper. Pour mixture into prepared casserole dish, pressing macaroni down in dish until submerged in liquid. Cover dish tightly with aluminum foil and bake for 20 minutes; remove from oven and stir. Return to oven and bake uncovered for 25 to 30 minutes longer or until pasta is fully cooked, stirring again partway through cooking time. Let stand 10 minutes before serving.

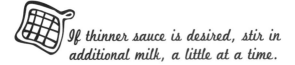
If thinner sauce is desired, stir in additional milk, a little at a time.

Easy Cheesy Lasagna

Ingredients

1 C. diced onion
1 tsp. minced garlic
2 (15 oz.) cans tomato sauce
2 C. sliced mushrooms
1 C. tomato juice
¼ C. chopped fresh basil
1 (15 oz.) container ricotta cheese
1 egg

½ tsp. salt
¼ tsp. pepper
10 no-boil lasagna noodles (6 to 7 oz.), divided
3 to 4 C. shredded mozzarella cheese, divided
1 C. grated Parmesan cheese, divided

Preparation

Preheat oven to 350°. In a large bowl, combine onion, garlic, tomato sauce, mushrooms, tomato juice and basil; set aside. In a small bowl, mix ricotta cheese, egg, salt and pepper; set aside.

Spread 1½ cups sauce mixture over bottom of an ungreased 9 x 13" baking dish. In layers, top sauce mixture with half the uncooked lasagna noodles, all the ricotta mixture, half the mozzarella cheese, ½ cup Parmesan cheese, 1½ cups sauce mixture and remaining lasagna noodles. Spread remaining sauce mixture over noodles and sprinkle with remaining mozzarella and Parmesan cheeses. Cover dish tightly with aluminum foil that has been sprayed with nonstick cooking spray. Bake for 45 minutes. Remove foil and bake 15 minutes longer or until lightly browned. Remove from oven and let stand about 15 minutes before cutting to serve.

Quick Mexican Bake

serves 4

Ingredients

¾ C. Mexican-style stewed tomatoes with juice

1½ T. plus 1 C. biscuit baking mix, divided

¾ C. frozen vegetarian chicken strips,* thawed

1 (15.5 oz.) can light red kidney beans, rinsed and drained

¾ C. frozen corn

6 T. milk

3 T. egg substitute

Preparation

Preheat oven to 400°. Grease a 1½-quart microwave-safe baking dish with nonstick cooking spray. Drain tomatoes, pouring the juice into prepared baking dish. Add 1½ tablespoons baking mix to juice and whisk to blend. Dice vegetarian chicken strips and tomato pieces; add to juice mixture. Stir in kidney beans and corn. Cover and microwave on high power for 3 minutes; stir.

Meanwhile, in a small bowl, combine remaining 1 cup baking mix with milk and egg substitute; whisk together until blended. Pour over tomato mixture in baking dish. Bake uncovered in oven for 25 to 35 minutes or until golden brown.

* Such as Morning Star or Lightlife products. This dish may also be prepared using diced cooked chicken.

Spinach-Tomato Pasta Casserole

serves 6

Ingredients

2 C. uncooked whole wheat rigatoni or macaroni

3 T. olive oil

2 C. shredded white Cheddar cheese

4 oz. fontina cheese

1 C. chopped fresh or frozen spinach, thawed

½ C. chopped tomatoes

4 oz. cream cheese

3¾ to 4 C. milk

1 tsp. prepared yellow mustard

Salt and pepper to taste

Preparation

Preheat oven to 350°. In an ungreased 9 x 13" baking dish, toss uncooked pasta and olive oil until coated. Spread pasta in a single layer in bottom of dish. Without stirring, sprinkle Cheddar and fontina cheeses over pasta. Arrange spinach and tomatoes evenly over cheeses. Cut cream cheese into very small pieces and scatter on top of vegetables; set aside.

In a medium bowl, whisk together milk and mustard. Season with salt and pepper as desired. Carefully pour milk mixture over casserole to cover pasta without displacing ingredients. Bake for 45 to 55 minutes or until pasta is tender and top is golden brown. Let stand 5 to 10 minutes before serving.

Sweet Potato Tortilla Bake

serves 6

Ingredients

4 (9") whole wheat tortillas
1 (15 oz.) can sweet potatoes, drained
1 (15 oz.) can black beans, rinsed and drained
1 C. chunky tomato salsa, divided

2 tsp. chili powder
1 (14 oz.) can tomato sauce
1 C. shredded Cheddar cheese
1 ripe avocado, peeled and pitted
¼ C. finely chopped green onion
½ C. sour cream

Preparation

Preheat oven to 450°. Grease a 9 x 13" baking dish with nonstick cooking spray. Cut tortillas into quarters. Arrange half of tortilla pieces in bottom of prepared dish. In a medium bowl, mash sweet potatoes. Add black beans, ½ cup salsa and chili powder; mix well. Spread bean mixture over tortillas in pan. Arrange remaining tortilla pieces over top; set aside.

In a small bowl, combine tomato sauce and remaining ½ cup salsa. Pour mixture evenly over tortillas. Bake uncovered for 15 to 20 minutes. Remove from oven and sprinkle cheese on top. Let stand about 5 minutes to melt cheese. Dice avocado. Garnish servings with avocado, green onion and a dollop of sour cream.

Overnight Meatless Manicotti

serves 7

Ingredients

12 oz. frozen ground beef or sausage substitute,* thawed
1½ C. cottage cheese
½ C. shredded mozzarella cheese
¼ C. shredded Parmesan cheese

1 (8 oz.) pkg. uncooked manicotti shells
24 to 26 oz. spaghetti sauce
½ C. shredded Colby Jack cheese

Preparation

Grease a 9 x 13" baking dish with nonstick cooking spray; set aside. In a large bowl, combine uncooked meat substitute, cottage cheese, mozzarella cheese and Parmesan cheese until well blended. Stuff a portion of mixture into each uncooked manicotti shell. Arrange shells in prepared baking dish. Pour spaghetti sauce over all. Cover dish tightly with aluminum foil and refrigerate overnight.

When ready to bake, preheat oven to 350°. Bake covered for 1 hour or until hot and bubbly. Remove from oven and sprinkle Colby Jack cheese over top. Return to oven and bake uncovered 5 to 10 minutes longer or until cheese is melted. Let stand 5 to 10 minutes before serving.

* Such as sausage-flavored crumbles from Gimme Lean, Morning Star or other brands.

Greek-Style Pizza

serves 8

Ingredients

2 T. melted butter
1 T. olive oil
3 T. minced garlic
2 T. sun-dried tomato pesto
1 T. chopped fresh basil
1 tsp. dried oregano
3 T. grated Parmesan cheese, divided

1 ready-to-bake pizza crust
1 roma tomato
1 bunch fresh spinach
1 sweet onion
1 jalapeño pepper, seeded
1 (6 oz.) container crumbled feta cheese

Preparation

Preheat oven according to pizza crust package directions. In a small bowl, combine melted butter, olive oil, garlic, pesto, basil, oregano and 1 tablespoon Parmesan cheese. Mix well and spread evenly on pizza crust.

Thinly slice tomato and drain on paper towels. Tear spinach leaves. Dice onion and jalapeño pepper. Arrange tomato, spinach, onion and jalapeño over sauce on crust. Top with feta cheese and remaining 2 tablespoons Parmesan cheese. Bake according to directions on pizza crust package. Slice into wedges or squares to serve.

Pierogies Parmigiana

serves 4

Ingredients

24 to 26 oz. spaghetti sauce
12 oz. frozen potato and
  cheese pierogies
1 (8 to 9 oz.) pkg. frozen sugar
  snap peas

1 tsp. dried Italian seasoning
½ C. grated Parmesan cheese
½ C. shredded mozzarella cheese

Preparation

Preheat oven to 375°. Grease a 2-quart casserole dish with nonstick cooking spray. In prepared dish, combine spaghetti sauce, frozen pierogies, snap peas and Italian seasoning, stirring until well coated. Cover dish tightly with aluminum foil and bake for 35 to 40 minutes or until pierogies are hot and edges of casserole are bubby. Remove from oven and top with Parmesan and mozzarella cheeses. Return to oven and bake uncovered for 5 to 10 minutes, until cheeses begin to brown.

Meatless

Spinach-Feta Pita Rounds

serves 6

Ingredients

1 (6 oz.) container sun-dried
tomato pesto
6 (6") whole wheat pita breads
2 roma tomatoes
1 bunch fresh spinach

4 fresh mushrooms
½ C. crumbled feta cheese
2 T. grated Parmesan cheese
3 T. olive oil
Pepper to taste

Preparation

Preheat oven to 350°. Spread some tomato pesto on one side
of each pita bread round. Arrange rounds, pesto side up, on an
ungreased cookie sheet; set aside.

Chop tomatoes and spinach; slice mushrooms. Top pita rounds with
tomato slices, a generous amount of spinach, mushrooms and feta
cheese. Sprinkle Parmesan cheese on top and drizzle with olive oil.
Season with pepper. Bake for 12 minutes or until pita breads are
crisp. Cut into quarters and serve.

Next Day Ravioli

serves 12

Ingredients

2 (9 oz.) pkgs. refrigerated four
  cheese ravioli
4 to 6 oz. oil-packed dried
  tomatoes, drained
1½ C. shredded Cheddar cheese
1½ C. shredded Monterey
  Jack cheese

½ C. grated Parmesan cheese
8 eggs, beaten
2½ C. milk
2 tsp. chopped fresh basil
  or parsley

Preparation

Grease a 9 x 13" baking dish or 3-quart casserole dish with nonstick cooking spray. Arrange uncooked ravioli evenly in prepared baking dish. Chop tomatoes and place on top of ravioli. Top with Cheddar, Monterey Jack and Parmesan cheeses; set aside.

In a large bowl, whisk together eggs and milk until well blended. Pour egg mixture over ingredients in baking dish. Cover tightly and refrigerate overnight.

When ready to bake, preheat oven to 350°. Uncover dish and bake approximately 40 minutes or until top is golden and center is set. Remove from oven and let stand 10 minutes. Sprinkle with basil just before serving.

Variation
For a meaty version, use beef ravioli instead of cheese ravioli.

Mock Chicken Enchiladas

serves 6

Ingredients

1 (8 oz.) pkg. frozen vegetarian chicken strips,* partially thawed

1 (10 oz.) pkg. frozen chopped spinach, thawed and drained

½ C. sliced green onions

2 C. light sour cream

½ C. plain yogurt

¼ C. flour

½ tsp. salt

Pepper to taste

1 tsp. ground cumin

1 C. milk

2 (4 oz.) cans diced green chiles

12 (6" to 7") flour tortillas

⅔ C. shredded Monterey Jack or Cheddar cheese

Snipped fresh cilantro

Fresh tomato salsa or picante sauce

Preparation

Preheat oven to 350°. Dice vegetarian chicken strips and place in a large bowl. Stir in spinach and green onions; set aside. Lightly grease a 9 x 13" baking dish with nonstick cooking spray; set aside.

In a large bowl, whisk together sour cream, yogurt, flour, salt, pepper and cumin. Stir in milk and chiles. Divide mixture in half. Pour one portion of sauce mixture into chicken mixture and stir well. Spoon a portion of chicken filling on each tortilla and roll up. Place filled tortillas, seam side down, in prepared baking dish. Spread remaining sauce mixture over tortilla rolls. Bake uncovered for 35 to 40 minutes or until bubbly and lightly browned on top. Remove from oven and sprinkle with cheese; let stand 5 minutes to melt cheese. Sprinkle with cilantro and serve with salsa.

* Such as Morning Star or Lightlife products. This dish may also be prepared using diced cooked chicken.

Baking times are listed in parentheses. Prep and standing times are not included.

Bakes less than 1 hour

Beef

Pork

Poultry

Seafood

Eggs

Meatless

Bakes about 1 hour

Beef

Bakes 1 to 2 hours

Bakes 2 to 4 hours

Refrigerated overnight, bakes next day